SECOND EDITION

IN CHARGE 2 WORKBOOK

An Integrated Skills Course for High-Level Students

Deborah Gordon

Consulting authors
James E. Purpura
Diane Pinkley

LONGMAN ON THE **WEB**

Longman.com offers online resources for teachers and students. Access our Companion Websites, our online catalog, and our local offices around the world.

Longman English Success offers online courses to give learners flexible study options. Courses cover General English, Business English, and Exam Preparation.

Visit us at **longman.com** and **englishsuccess.com**.

Longman

In Charge 2 Workbook, Second Edition

Pearson Education, 10 Bank Street, White Plains, NY 10606

Vice president of instructional design: Allen Ascher
Editorial manager: Pam Fishman
Project manager: Margaret Grant
Development editor: Debbie Lazarus
Vice president, director of design and production: Rhea Banker
Executive managing editor: Linda Moser
Production manager: Liza Pleva
Production coordinator: Melissa Leyva
Production editor/Reprint manager: Robert Ruvo
Director of manufacturing: Patrice Fraccio
Senior manufacturing buyer: Edie Pullman
Photo research: Aerin Csigay
Cover design: Tracey Cataldo
Text composition: Design 5 Creatives
Text font: 11/14 Palatino
Illustrations: Susan Detrich, pp. 13, 17, 25, 26, 33, 49, 50, 74, 83, 85;
    Tim Haggerty, pp. 1, 11, 18, 37, 69, 90; Lou Pappas, p. 44; Phil Scheuer,
    pp. 4, 9, 10, 21, 28, 41, 42, 45, 57, 60, 78, 81, 89, 92
Photo credits: p. 11 Pierre Burnaugh/PhotoEdit; p. 6 Billy E. Barnes/
    PhotoEdit; p. 19 Robert Brenner/PhotoEdit; p. 38 AP/Wide World Photos;
    p. 43 Roger Ressmeyer/Corbis; p. 52 Jeff Greenberg/PhotoEdit;
    p. 54 Michael Newman/PhotoEdit; p. 59 Jonathan Nourok/PhotoEdit;
    p. 61 Robert Pickett/Corbis; p. 62 Spencer Grant/PhotoEdit; p. 67 Deborah
    Lazarus-Yarzagaray; p. 70 Peter Johnson/Corbis; p. 75 AP/Wide World
    Photos; p. 77 Bettmann/Corbis; p. 84 David Young-Wolff/PhotoEdit.

ISBN 0-13-094381-9

Printed in the United States of America
3 4 5 6 7 8 9 10 11-VHG-10 09 08 07

BUYER BEWARE

PRACTICE 1

Do you sometimes find yourself humming an advertising jingle (song) even when you don't like the ad or jingle? Think of an advertising jingle and the product it is attempting to sell. Work in small groups and take turns humming your jingles.

- Try to guess what ad each student's jingle is from.
- Tell each other what you like or don't like about the ad.
- Discuss whether you think the ad is effective or not.

PRACTICE 2

Unscramble the vocabulary words. Then complete the sentences about multicultural advertising mistakes. Refer to page 4 in your student book for help.

a. nmndrsseeoet _____   **e.** otersystepe _____

b. iscmal _____   **f.** inutehcla _____

c. glaons _____   **g.** mikgmci _____

d. crleyebit _____

1. A well-known fast-food chain was upset to find that in China its _____, "finger lickin' good," translated as "eat your fingers off."

2. A cola company also had problems in China when they discovered they were making impossible _____ with their "brings you back to life" ad campaign because it was translated as "It brings your ancestors back from the grave."

3. Products that use famous names and faces in their advertising campaigns may not be effective unless they get local _____ _____.

4. For example, the milk industry's _____ of using famous faces with milk mustaches just wouldn't have the same effect in countries where those faces aren't famous.

5. Although in the United States and Canada many people consider the advertising of cigarettes to be _____, the Japanese probably just laughed at the cigarette campaign that was translated as "When smoking our cigarettes, you feel so refreshed that your mind seems to be free and empty."

6. The idea that girls are not good in math is an example of a negative _____.

PRACTICE 3

A. Two friends are in a mall shopping. Work with a partner. Complete the conversation.

ROLES	CONVERSATION	FUNCTIONS
Antonio:	Wow! These are really great DVDs. I wish I could buy some of them.	State a wish.
Trina:	Why don't you? They're on sale. Did you bring enough money? Do you have a DVD player?	Ask for details.
Antonio:	Well, actually I haven't bought a DVD player yet. I'm waiting until _____ _____.	Elaborate.
Trina:	Since we're already in the store, let's go check out the _____ _____.	Give a recommendation and a reason for using a product.

B. Take turns being the two friends and give recommendations on the following products:

- **a.** portable CD player
- **b.** handheld organizer
- **c.** digital camera
- **d.** (your own idea)

PRACTICE 4

A. Complete the following ad by writing either *as . . . as* or *so . . . as* in the blanks.

It's _____ gentle _____ a summer breeze. And even though it's all natural, it's just _____ strong _____ the other brands. It's concentrated, however, so you won't need to use _____ much _____ you do with the other brands, and it isn't _____ expensive _____ the other brands. Also, because it's all natural, you won't need to worry _____ much _____ you do with the other brands about how much you use. It's completely safe for people, the environment, and your clothes.

B. With a partner, decide what product is being advertised in Part A.

A. Read this list of criteria for writing effective print ads. Complete the sentences with words from the box.

enough	such	so	very	too

1. Ideas must be expressed _____ clearly that no questions remain.

2. Although it is acceptable to use compound and complex sentences, it is critical that these sentences not contain _____ many ideas.

3. There should be precisely just _____ ideas in each sentence to retain clarity.

4. A common failure in print ads is that sentences are not written concisely _____ .

5. While repetition is acceptable, and can even be desirable at times, redundancy can be a _____ costly mistake.

6. Ads that are lighthearted and humorous are also desirable, but they must never be _____ humorous for the purpose of the message.

7. The purpose of an ad has _____ importance that much time and effort are spent on making sure it is expressed clearly.

B. Work in small groups. Look through magazines and newspapers to find ads that illustrate some of the points mentioned in Part A. Give reasons for your choices.

PRACTICE 6

A. Read each numbered sentence and check the statement that best describes it.

1. The new iced tea ad isn't as effective as the old one, which had all the dancing.
   - ☐ The dancing iced tea ad doesn't work as well as the new ad.
   - ☐ The dancing iced tea ad works better than the new ad.

2. Online advertising usually isn't as expensive as TV advertising.
   - ☐ TV advertising is usually more expensive than online advertising.
   - ☐ Online advertising isn't usually cheaper than TV advertising.

3. The volume of visitor hits to that online banner ad wasn't high enough.
   - ☐ That online banner ad wasn't getting such a large number of visitor hits.
   - ☐ The volume of visitor hits to that online banner ad was as high as desired.

(continued on next page)

4. The industry-wide advertising slowdown didn't affect magazines as much as newspapers.

☐ Newspapers were hit harder than magazines by the advertising slowdown.

☐ Newspapers weren't affected more than magazines by the industry-wide advertising slowdown.

5. Some ads say as much without words as others say with words.

☐ Ads without words usually don't say enough.

☐ Ads with words don't always say more than those without words.

B. Compare your answers with a partner's. Then find new ways to say the same thing as each numbered sentence. Use the comparatives *as . . . as, so . . . as, not such, not so,* and *enough.*

PRACTICE 7

Work with a partner. Compare the two magazine ads below. Talk about the effectiveness of the ads, the possible target audiences, and the costs to produce the ads. Give reasons for your opinions. Include the following structures in your discussion: *as . . . as, so . . . as, so, such, enough, very, so, too.* Use the language from the box.

Language for Expressing Opinions

I think that . . .

In my opinion . . .

I feel . . .

I'm not sure I agree with you about... because...

If you ask me...

PRACTICE 8

A.   Before You Listen Discuss these questions in small groups. How do you let people know what you are feeling? What specific feelings can you communicate with your voice?

B. Listen to three ads. Write the product each ad is advertising.

1. _____

2. _____

3. _____

C. Listen to the ads again. Pay attention to the speakers' tone of voice and check the appropriate boxes. Then compare your answers with a partner's.

	Ad 1	Ad 2	Ad 3
suspicious			
grateful			
sarcastic			
disappointed			
surprised			
enthusiastic			

PRACTICE 9

A. Identify the thought groups with a slash (/). Predict which syllables are stressed in each group. Draw a line under those syllables.

You know, sometimes I really wonder about the things they put on product labels. I mean, have you ever looked at a milk or juice carton and wondered why you had to open it on one side instead of the other? Is the glue on one side different from the glue on the other? Or how about the reminder on those strips of dried fruit not to eat the plastic wrapping, or the one that tells us to cook the frozen food before eating it? Who are these people who need these warnings anyway? I mean really. Do you know anyone who has mistaken a frozen dinner for an ice cream bar?

B. Listen to the passage to check your predictions.

C. Work with a partner. Take turns reading the passage aloud.

PRACTICE 10

A. List the important elements to remember in each aspect of a discussion.

1. Introducing a discussion

greeting the attendees _____

_____

_____

_____

2. Organizing a discussion

_____

_____

_____

managing a discussion

3. Moving a discussion forward

_____

_____

_____

B. Work in small groups. Take turns managing a discussion on the following topics. Use the language from the box.

- Using the name of the competition in an advertisement

- Making false claims for your product

- Using persuasive advertising aimed at young children

- Reaching the teen market with your product

> **Language for Discussion Management**
> We'll focus on . . .
> Our most important task today is . . .
> We have fifteen minutes left to . . .
> Any more comments on . . . before we
>   move on to . . . ?
> Today we need to discuss . . .
> Our next topic of discussion is . . .
> Good point, but we need to move on to . . .

PRACTICE 11

A. Choose two topics from the box and imagine that you are going to write essays on them. Decide on an audience and a purpose for each one.

> **Example:** TOPIC: Billboard advertising
> AUDIENCE: City council
> PURPOSE: To persuade against having billboards

1. TOPIC _____

AUDIENCE _____

PURPOSE _____

2. TOPIC _____

AUDIENCE _____

PURPOSE _____

> **Topics**
> - Political campaign advertising
> - Stereotyping
> - Advertising's influence on young people
> - Banning alcohol and tobacco advertising
> - (your own idea)

B. Work in groups. Take turns sharing your topics and audience. Ask the other group members to guess your purpose.

C. Choose one of your topics and write the opening paragraph below. Focus on your specific audience and purpose.

YOU'RE IN CHARGE!

UNIT ONE OBJECTIVES: How well did you meet the objectives for this unit?
Check the box next to each objective you feel you mastered.

GRAMMAR
- ❏ Comparatives: *as . . . as, so . . . as*
- ❏ Sufficiency: *enough*
- ❏ Intensifiers: *very, so, such, too*
- ❏ Unequal comparisons: *not so, not such, not as.*

LISTENING
- ❏ Listening for tone

SPEAKING
Reviewing discussion skills (1):
- ❏ Introducing a discussion
- ❏ Organizing a discussion
- ❏ Moving a discussion forward

PRONUNCIATION
- ❏ Rhythm and thought groups

READING
- ❏ Skimming to find key ideas

WRITING
- ❏ Developing a clear sense of topic
- ❏ Considering the audience
- ❏ Maintaining a clear purpose

LEARNING STRATEGIES: Reflect on your use of learning strategies and thinking skills in this unit. What are some of the strategies you employed? Which ones were most successful for you?

Write your thoughts here.

_____
_____
_____
_____
_____
_____
_____
_____
_____

Unit 1 Learning Strategies
- Using context to determine meaning
- Comparing
- Categorizing
- Taking notes
- Making predictions
- Skimming
- Working cooperatively

Look at the picture of two people dreaming. Work with a partner to decide on a possible interpretation for each of the dreams. Join with another pair and compare your interpretations. Give reasons for your decisions. Is either of the dreams similar to the types of dreams you have?

Complete the crossword puzzle. Refer to page 16 in your student book for help.

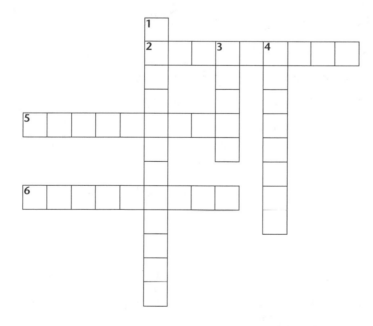

ACROSS

2. descendants
5. those with serious problems or disease
6. accurately predicting the future

DOWN

1. occurring at the same time by accident
3. shelter from the heat and sunlight
4. cured, corrected

A. A psychologist and a patient are talking about the patient's dreams. Work with a partner. Complete the conversation.

ROLES	CONVERSATION	FUNCTIONS
Patient:	Last night I had a very frightening dream. I dreamed I was in my bed and there was something terrible coming at me.	Talk about a dream.
Psychologist:	Do you remember anything else?	Ask for details.
Patient:	_____ _____ What do you think it means?	Give details and request an interpretation.
Psychologist:	Perhaps you were anxious about something that is about to happen to you. Or maybe you _____.	Give two possible interpretations.

B. Take turns being the psychologist and the patient and talk about the following dreams.

    a. I was at a party but no one recognized me.

    b. I received a letter saying I had gotten an inheritance.

    c. I was trying to catch a plane but everything was going wrong.

    d. I was riding on the back of a dolphin.

    e. (your own idea)

PRACTICE 4

Decide if the following sentences need *either . . . or* or *neither . . . nor*. Write them above where they belong, adding insert marks.

                          either   *or*

    Example: It seems that people ⌃ have no problem remembering their dreams ⌃ they remember very few, if any at all.

    1. To remember your dreams, put a large note saying "DREAMS" where you will see it as soon as you wake up keep a journal near your bed.

2. As soon as you realize you are awake, it is important that you move much start thinking about anything specific apart from things to do with your dreams.

3. As you begin to remember your dreams, it is essential that you write down record on your cassette recorder everything you can remember about your dreams.

4. If these methods don't work for you at first, you should get upset give up on this idea. Sometimes it just takes persistence.

PRACTICE 5

A. Complete the passage with the correct words from the box. Use each word only once.

and	if
as long as	in addition to
unless	for example
or	otherwise

Because Sigmund Freud had no knowledge of REM sleep, he theorized that **(1.)** _____ dreams had a function, it must be to keep people from waking up too early. **(2.)** _____ how would people get enough sleep each night? Freud's theory was that **(3.)** _____ people's minds were engaged in dreams, the slightest noises **(4.)** _____ their own thoughts might prevent them from staying asleep.

Once psychologists knew about REM sleep, they began to gather evidence that dreaming happened multiple times, perhaps five or six times, during REM sleep. It became clear that dreams must have other functions **(5.)** _____ simply keeping people from waking too early. Then psychologists discovered that dreams occur both during REM

(6.) _____ outside of REM sleep. Many psychologists were more convinced than ever that dreaming fulfilled an important function. Some psychologists, **(7.)** _____, believe that we dream to help us solve our problems. However, other psychologists disagree. It is their opinion that **(8.)** _____ we remember only a very small percentage of our dreams, dreaming probably has no real function at all.

B. Compare your answers with a partner's and explain your choices.

PRACTICE 6

Complete the following sentences with information of your own. Then share your sentences with the class.

1. I rarely have nightmares. Moreover, _____
   _____.

2. People dream in color, but it is thought that animals, such as _____
   _____.

3. Those who interpret their dreams feel that dreams are particularly helpful in discovering more about their own feelings and _____.

4. Some people feel that interpreting their dreams helps them to resolve their problems. For example, _____
   _____.

5. People who have to be creative in their work, such as _____ sometimes report using their dreams as a source of ideas.

6. It is critical that everyone get enough deep sleep nightly to be able to dream. Otherwise,_____.

PRACTICE 7

Rewrite the following sentences using the words in parentheses. Make any necessary changes while keeping the meaning the same.

Example: I have bad dreams in the morning unless I get up before 7:00. **(otherwise)**
  I get up before 7:00; otherwise, I have bad dreams in the morning.

1. As long as I don't think about my work just before falling asleep, I usually sleep all right. **(unless)**

   _____

2. I can't go to sleep on a full stomach or I'll have nightmares. **(if)**

   _____

3. My brother sleeps so heavily that I don't think he'd wake up during an earthquake. **(in the event that)**

   _____

4. To ensure that I have good dreams at night, I make my last thoughts humorous ones. In addition, I listen to nice music. **(besides)**

_____

5. Sofia's little daughter doesn't have nightmares if she sleeps with her magic key. **(as long as)**

_____

PRACTICE 8

A. **Before You Listen** Discuss these questions in small groups. What types of things do you dream about most often? Can you think of any dreams that have helped you with new ideas or warned you about something?

You are getting sleepy. You are getting very sleepy.

B. Listen to two friends talk about dreaming. As you listen, identify each speaker's feelings about controlling dreams and the reasons for their feelings. Write your information on the chart. Then compare your answers with a partner's.

	Good or Bad Idea?	Reason 1	Reason 2	Reason 3
Pedro				
Sandra				

C. Work with a partner. Discuss these questions.

1. Do you think it would be a good or bad idea to control your dreams? Would you be able to do it?

2. How can you make your dreams work for you?

PRACTICE 9

A. Predict which words will be linked and reduced in each conversation and circle them. Check (✔) if the tone is formal or informal.

1. KEN: I bet different professions have different kinds (of) bad dreams.

TED: Probably. My bad dreams (have) always been about not being able to find my classroom.

KEN: That sounds like a typical nightmare for a teacher.

TED: What are yours?

KEN: Mine have often been about not being able to find the figures I need to give my sales report

TED: Then what happens?

KEN: I get fired, of course.

☐ FORMAL   ☐ INFORMAL

2. CAITLIN'S FRIEND: Caitlin, I'd like you to meet Dr. Cruz. She's an expert on different types of dream therapies. Dr. Cruz, this is Caitlin Oakley.

DR. CRUZ: Hello, Caitlin. Nice to meet you.

CAITLIN: Nice to meet you, too, Dr. Cruz. Do you mind if I ask you some questions for my article?

DR. CRUZ: Not at all. Please have a seat.

☐ FORMAL   ☐ INFORMAL

B. Listen to the conversations to check your predictions.

C. Work with a partner. Take turns reading the two conversations aloud.

PRACTICE 10

Although dreams may refer to thoughts, images, and emotions that occur during sleep, the word *dream* also means a strongly desired goal or ambition. Work in small groups. Take turns managing a discussion on the following topics:

- How to achieve your goals
- The best careers for the future
- Work or continue your education— which is better?

After introducing the discussion topic and purpose, remember to keep the following in mind:

- take turns
- stay on track
- clarify miscommunications

> **Language for Discussion Management**
>
> _____, we still haven't heard from you.
>
> _____, you have the floor now.
>
> Sorry to cut you short, _____, but we don't have much time left.
>
> I think we'd better get back to the topic at hand.
>
> To rephrase what I think you just said . . .
>
> What I meant to say was . . .

PRACTICE 11

A. Read the following essay test topics. Decide on possible purposes for each one from the list below:

ESSAY TOPICS

1. The history of dream therapy

Essay Purposes: _____

2. Lucid dreaming

Essay Purposes: _____

3. Benefits of dream therapy for young children

Essay Purposes: _____

4. Research on animal dreaming

Essay Purposes: _____

5. The differences between men's and women's dreams

Essay Purposes: _____

ESSAY PURPOSES

a. cause and effect

b. comparison and contrast

c. definition

d. exemplification

e. description

f. argumentation

g. summary

B. Work in groups. Take turns sharing your purposes. Give reasons for your choices.

YOU'RE IN CHARGE!

UNIT TWO OBJECTIVES: How well did you meet the objectives for this unit? Check the box next to each objective you feel you mastered.

GRAMMAR

- ❑ *either . . . or, neither . . . nor*
- ❑ Using connectors such as transitional devices, prepositions, and conjunctions

LISTENING

- ❑ Listening for personal interpretation

SPEAKING

Reviewing discussion skills (2):
- ❑ Taking turns
- ❑ Staying on track
- ❑ Clarifying miscommunications

PRONUNCIATION

- ❑ Linking and reduction of words

READING

- ❑ Previewing a reading passage

WRITING

- ❑ Responding to essay questions

LEARNING STRATEGIES: Reflect on your use of learning strategies and thinking skills in this unit. What are some of the strategies you employed? Which ones were most successful for you?

Write your thoughts here.

_____

_____

_____

_____

_____

_____

_____

_____

_____

Unit 2 Learning Strategies
- Using context to determine meaning
- Using prior knowledge
- Classifying
- Analyzing
- Taking notes
- Skimming
- Predicting
- Working cooperatively

PRACTICE 1

Look at the picture and discuss these questions with a partner.

- Two U.S. laws are being broken. What do you think they are? (Answer on page 21.)

- Are there laws governing these actions in your home country?

- Do you think these actions should be against the law? Why or why not?

- What do you think the fines or punishments should be?

PRACTICE 2

Complete the paragraph with words from the box.

noted	codes of conduct	take precedence	means	elderly

The lives of the (1.) _____ are affected by laws and regulations. However, recently the rights of the elderly have started to (2.) _____ with lawmakers because of the rapid growth of the senior citizen population. Modern medicine and awareness of health are giving elderly people the (3.) _____ to live longer. Consequently, lawmakers are writing new (4.) _____ to deal with increasing numbers of senior citizens. Many (5.) _____ senior citizens are challenging laws that need changing. For example, laws about mandatory retirement seem inappropriate when many senior citizens prefer to continue working and are physically able to do so.

PRACTICE 3

A. Two law students are talking about an exam they are going to take soon. Work with a partner. Complete the conversation.

Roles	Conversation	Functions
Carl:	I think we've covered all the main topics that are going to be on the test, haven't we?	Ask for confirmation of a statement.
Yolanda:	Yes/No, _____.	Confirm or deny the statement.
Carl:	You know what room the exam's in, don't you?	Ask a related question.
Yolanda:	Yes/No, _____.	Confirm or deny.

B. Take turns being the law students and discuss these topics.

   a. a presentation you are working on together

   b. a guest speaker coming to the class

   c. a study date you are making before the next exam

   d. a topic from the class that you don't understand

   e. (your own idea)

PRACTICE 4

A. Complete the conversation with the appropriate tag questions.

HOST: Today I'm talking with Gillian Watson, an authority on archaic laws still in existence. Gillian, by archaic you mean old and not used anymore, **(1.)** _____?

GILLIAN: That's right, Marco. And I bet you're going to ask me how I got started, **(2.)** _____?

HOST: You read my mind.

GILLIAN: Well, sometimes you just need to look at the humorous side of something as serious as the law, so my scholarly studies just took me in that direction.

HOST: OK, Gillian, I think we're ready to hear a few humorous examples. You've got a law about alligators, **(3.)** _____?

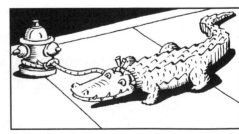

GILLIAN: Yes. This is a good one. I bet you didn't know that in one of the U.S. southern states there's a law that you can't tie up an alligator to a fire hydrant.

HOST: No, I can't imagine anyone being aware of that one, **(4.)** _____?
And it's not going to come up in court any time soon, **(5.)** _____?

GILLIAN: *(laugh)* No, I don't believe so. While I'm on the subject of wildlife, here's another strange law. In one place I know of, it's illegal to annoy birds! Of course, birds wouldn't exactly complain now, **(6.)** _____?

HOST: Those kinds of laws aren't so bad though, **(7.)** _____? I mean, those laws protect the wildlife, and if someone is throwing stones at birds, for example, the police could do something about it, **(8.)** _____?

GILLIAN: You've got a point there, Marco. I guess we should keep that one on the law books, **(9.)** _____?

B. Compare your answers with a partner's and explain your choices.

PRACTICE 5

Rewrite the sentences using initial participial phrases. Make other changes as needed. If the adverb clause cannot be reduced, write **No Change**.

Example:

Because animal rights activists were so concerned about the treatment of animals, they appealed to law schools to teach a course in animal rights law.

Being so concerned about the treatment of animals, animal
rights activists appealed to law schools to teach a special
course in animal rights law.

1. Before two professors wrote their own animal rights law course, they searched law school programs to see if there was one already written.

_____

_____

2. As they couldn't find any courses already written, they had to write their own.

_____

_____

3. While one northeastern U.S. law school has been teaching an animal rights law course since 1990, other universities have only recently gotten started doing the same.

_____

_____

4. Since people have become aware of the need for more laws protecting the rights of animals, they have started opening animal rights foundations.

_____

_____

PRACTICE 6

A. Cross out the words that are incorrectly placed in the boxes below. Then choose two expressions from each box and work with a partner to write sentences.

Expressions of Contrast	
although	however
on the other hand	but
despite	nontheless
whereas	while

Expressions of Concession	
yet	but
while	in spite of
however	even so
on the other hand	in contrast

B. Share your sentences with another pair of students.

PRACTICE 7

A. Complete the sentences with an appropriate expression of contrast or concession.

1. Many laws are written to protect people. _____, these same laws can actually hinder the progress of the people they were written to protect.

2. _____ there are laws which are meant to protect animals, they don't actually provide animals with rights.

3. No one believed he was innocent _____his being found not guilty in court.

4. _____ newspapers are protected by free speech rights, libel laws protect individuals from having lies printed in newspapers.

5. Some laws written ages ago are still relevant; _____, other very old laws need to be changed.

6. Surveillance cameras in buildings and on streets violate people's right to privacy. _____, many people feel that it is worth the loss of privacy to have increased safety.

7. _____ many criminals are caught and sent to prison, they are rarely given an opportunity to meet their victims and take responsibility for their actions.

8. The city government was slow to change its building codes _____ pressure from many senior citizen groups.

B. Compare your answers with a partner's and explain your choices.

PRACTICE 8

A. Before You Listen Discuss these questions in small groups. Why are courtroom dramas and mysteries so popular? Do they interest you? If so, which ones?

🎧 **B.** Listen to the conversation between friends. Write the analogies that Jae uses to describe the following:

The courtroom suspense: _____

_____

_____

Tom Krishna: _____

_____

Lena Berry's questioning technique: _____

_____

Watching Lena Berry: _____

_____

Opening night: _____

_____

C. Listen again. Answer the following questions and compare your answers with a partner's.

1. What is the name of the movie Jae wants to see?

   _____

2. What kind of movie does Melvin want to see?

   _____

3. Why doesn't Melvin want to see the same movie as Jae?

   _____

4. Who does he recommend that Jae invite to the movies?

   _____

5. When you go to movies, do you want to see things that are the same as or different from your daily life? Why?

   _____

Answer to Practice 1: U.S. laws broken are (1) littering and (2) driving without seat belts buckled.

A. Predict the speakers' intonation in the following conversation by drawing a rising arrow ⬈ or a falling arrow ⬊ over each tag question.

JOSH: Hey, what did you think of the speaker we had in class today? She had some interesting ideas, didn't she?

AHMED: Yeah, I guess so. But I'm still not sure I understand restorative justice. It's fairly new, isn't it?

JOSH: Not really. I think it started in Canada about thirty years ago. Victims have a chance to speak with the offender or criminal person who harmed them. And it lets the offender hear the victim's point of view. They also call it Victim-Offender Mediation. That's right, isn't it Monica?

MONICA: Right, Josh. It also provides a chance for the offenders to take responsibility for their actions. To make it right, so to speak, with the victims. If you were a victim of a crime, you'd want to tell the criminal how you feel, wouldn't you? I know I would.

AHMED: But if I were dead, I wouldn't be able to, now would I?

JOSH: That's true. But there might be family members of yours or other people in the community who would want to talk with the criminal. This would give them that chance in a safe situation, right?

AHMED: I think I understand. Victim-Offender Mediation isn't just about the law; it's also about trying to repair human relationships. You understand what I mean, don't you?

MONICA: Yeah, I do. Whether the victim and the offender knew each other before or not doesn't matter, does it?

JOSH: Well, I hope we get that speaker back again. But for now, let's go eat. I'm starving, aren't you?

B. Listen to the conversation to check your predictions.

C. Work in groups of three and read the conversation together.

PRACTICE 10

Work in small groups. Take turns discussing the following topics and trying
to reach a decision.

- Giving appropriate penalties for littering
- Limiting the amount that lawyers are
  permitted to charge their clients
- Requiring judges to retire at a certain age
- Maintaining lawyer-client confidentiality
  even when someone's life is at risk
- (Your own idea)

Remember to do the following when appropriate:

- propose a solution
- analyze a solution
- evade an answer
- offer support

Language for Decision Making

I'd like to offer a suggestion.
Don't you think that a better course
  of action might be . . .
How would it be if we . . .
I can see several problems that we
  should discuss.
Looking at the pros and cons of that . . .
Let's hear what Pedro has to offer.
I think you have a practical idea.

PRACTICE 11

A. Choose two topics on which to write opinion essays. Decide on your opinion and
whether to use a deductive or an inductive approach. Then fill in the information below.

1. TOPIC: _____

   Your opinion: _____

   _____

   _____

   APPROACH: _____

   Reason for approach: _____

   _____

2. TOPIC: _____

   Your opinion: _____

   _____

   _____

   APPROACH: _____

   Reason for approach: _____

   _____

Topics
- Should important trials be televised?
- Should a judge be appointed or
  voted on?
- Should animals have legal rights like
  humans do?
- Should all lawyers be required to do
  pro bono (free) work for defendants
  who can't afford to pay for a lawyer?

B. Work in small groups. Share your opinions and chosen approaches. Discuss your
supporting reasons.

YOU'RE IN CHARGE!

UNIT THREE OBJECTIVES: How well did you meet the objectives for this unit? Check the box next to each objective you feel you mastered.

GRAMMAR
- ❑ Tag questions
- ❑ Reducing clauses to participial phrases
- ❑ Expressions of contrast and concession

LISTENING
- ❑ Listening for analogies

SPEAKING
Reviewing discussion skills (3):
- ❑ Proposing a solution
- ❑ Analyzing a solution
- ❑ Evading an answer
- ❑ Offering support

PRONUNCIATION
- ❑ Intonation in tag questions

READING
- ❑ Categorizing examples

WRITING
- ❑ Writing an opinion essay
- ❑ Using a deductive approach
- ❑ Using an inductive approach

LEARNING STRATEGIES: Reflect on your use of learning strategies and thinking skills in this unit. What are some of the strategies you employed? Which ones were most successful for you?

Write your thoughts here.

_____

_____

_____

_____

_____

_____

_____

_____

_____

_____

Unit 3 Learning Strategies
- Using prior knowledge
- Using context to determine meaning
- Taking notes
- Making predictions
- Analyzing ideas
- Categorizing
- Working cooperatively

BEYOND WORDS

PRACTICE 1

Facial gestures are very important to understanding communication. Match the gestures with the pictures. Then work with a partner to decide on their meaning.

- **a.** raising eyebrows
- **b.** rolling eyes
- **c.** frowning
- **d.** wrinkling nose

PRACTICE 2

Complete the crossword puzzle. Refer to page 44 in your student book for help.

ACROSS

2. cruel; hurtful
5. cancels
6. sensing; understanding
7. borders; walls

DOWN

1. negates
3. erase; destroy
4. softened; smoothed

PRACTICE 3

A. A drama student is asking her drama coach how to express different emotions on stage. Work with a partner. Complete the conversation.

ROLES	CONVERSATION	FUNCTIONS
Mariko:	How can I show that I'm stressed out?	Ask about a gesture.
Ms. Sanders:	You could move around a lot. Grind your teeth, suck in air, and make angry noises.	Answer the question.
Mariko:	How about if I _____?	Ask about the appropriateness of another gesture.
Ms. Sanders:	Possibly. It depends on _____ _____.	Answer the question.

B. Take turns being the student and the drama coach. Discuss how to express these emotions.

    a. fear   **c.** boredom   **e.** (your own idea)

    b. annoyance   **d.** sadness

PRACTICE 4

Complete the following sentences with an appropriate form of the verbs in parentheses. Make any necessary changes.

Most people expect that gestures **(1. mean)** _____ the same thing in all cultures, but this **(2. could, not, be)** _____ farther from the truth. For example, while a simple head nod up and down in India **(3. would, interpret)** _____ as "yes," in Kuwait it **(4. would, mean)** _____ "no." Another gesture that **(5. could, easily, misunderstand)** _____ is when a woman from India **(6. touch)** _____ her nose with her forefinger to express surprise. This same gesture **(7. would, do)** _____ in the Middle East by a man to express his willingness to serve someone in whatever way he **(8. need)** _____. The willingness to serve in Iran **(9. would, express)** _____ by Irani people by covering their right eye with the palm of their right hand. While a wide smile showing teeth **(10. be)** _____ a sign of friendship and warmth to people from Western cultures, it **(11. can, consider)** _____ rude to people from some Asian cultures. Clearly, without sufficient knowledge, confusing or even offensive signals **(12. can, send)** _____ quite unintentionally.

PRACTICE 5

A. Read each numbered sentence and check the statement that best describes it.

1. Can I ask what you mean by that gesture?
   - ☐ Should I ask what you mean by that gesture?
   - ☐ Is it possible to ask what you mean by that gesture?

2. Could you understand what she was trying to communicate with her raised eyebrow?
   - ☐ Will you please try to understand what she was trying to tell us with her raised eyebrow?
   - ☐ Were you able to understand what she was trying to tell us with her raised eyebrow?

3. I should have taken that course in multicultural body language.
   - ☐ I expect that I will take that course in multicultural body language.
   - ☐ I regret that I didn't take that course in multicultural body language.

4. They must be offering that course again.
   - ☐ I think it is likely that they will be offering that course again.
   - ☐ I think they are required to offer that course again.

5. How could they have thought that my head nodding meant "no"?
   - ☐ I'm not sure if they thought I meant "no" by my head nod.
   - ☐ It seems impossible that they thought I meant "no" by my head nod.

6. You might ask her what she means when she puts up her palms like that.
   - ☐ I suggest that you ask her what she means when she puts up her palms like that.
   - ☐ I insist that you ask her what she means when she puts up her palms like that.

7. We should have been informed by now.
   - ☐ I expected them to have informed us already.
   - ☐ They regret that they didn't inform us already.

8. Paolo can't talk to Haridi without having at least one misunderstanding.
   - ☐ Paolo and Haridi don't have permission to talk to each other.
   - ☐ Paolo and Haridi don't have the ability to understand each other completely.

B. Compare your answers with a partner's. Discuss other possible ways to say the numbered sentences. Share your new sentences with the class.

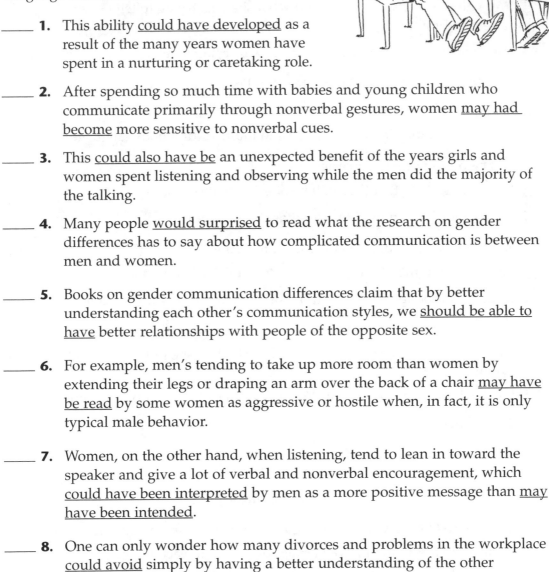

PRACTICE 6

A. Correct any mistakes in the underlined verb phrases. If the sentence is correct, put a check (✔) in front of it.

Example:

Research <u>has ~~been~~ found</u> that women are generally better at understanding body language than men are.

_____ **1.** This ability <u>could have developed</u> as a result of the many years women have spent in a nurturing or caretaking role.

_____ **2.** After spending so much time with babies and young children who communicate primarily through nonverbal gestures, women <u>may had become</u> more sensitive to nonverbal cues.

_____ **3.** This <u>could also have be</u> an unexpected benefit of the years girls and women spent listening and observing while the men did the majority of the talking.

_____ **4.** Many people <u>would surprised</u> to read what the research on gender differences has to say about how complicated communication is between men and women.

_____ **5.** Books on gender communication differences claim that by better understanding each other's communication styles, we <u>should be able to have</u> better relationships with people of the opposite sex.

_____ **6.** For example, men's tending to take up more room than women by extending their legs or draping an arm over the back of a chair <u>may have be read</u> by some women as aggressive or hostile when, in fact, it is only typical male behavior.

_____ **7.** Women, on the other hand, when listening, tend to lean in toward the speaker and give a lot of verbal and nonverbal encouragement, which <u>could have been interpreted</u> by men as a more positive message than <u>may have been intended</u>.

_____ **8.** One can only wonder how many divorces and problems in the workplace <u>could avoid</u> simply by having a better understanding of the other person's communication style.

B. Work with a partner to compare and explain your corrections.

PRACTICE 7

Work in small groups. Look around the room. Do you see any body language that you think is more typical of males or more typical of females? (If your class doesn't have both males and females, think about people you know and the way they sit, stand, and talk.) Fill in the following chart and then share your observations with the class. Use the language in the box to discuss possible interpretations.

> **Language for Discussing Possibilities**
>
> It's possible that . . .   She could be trying to express that . . .
> It seems like he may be . . .   It might be that . . .

Examples of Male Body Language	Examples of Female Body Language
	Women cross their legs in Western cultures

PRACTICE 8

A. Before You Listen Discuss the following question in small groups. Do you know any gestures that might be misunderstood by people not familiar with the culture the gesture comes from? Show your gestures to your group.

B. Listen to Greg and Chiaki talk about a meeting they just had with a group of Asian businesspeople. Fill in the chart with Greg and Chiaki's different opinions about some things that happened during the meeting. Compare your answers with a partner's.

Communication Acts	Greg's Interpretation	Chiaki's Interpretation
saying "yes"		
smiling when talking about money		
not maintaining eye contact		
not having strong handshakes		

C. Work in small groups. Discuss what advice you would give to Greg about communicating with people from your home country.

PRACTICE 9

A. Listen to the sentences. Circle the words in parentheses that you hear. Check your anwers with a partner's.

1. He should have taken the **(a. pill   b. bill)** later.
2. Did she use the old **(a. rope   b. robe)**?
3. We need some more **(a. wheat   b. heat)**.
4. She shouldn't have said **(a. "why"   b. "buy")**.
5. They must have bought a new **(a. fan   b. van)**.
6. They must have **(a. fought   b. thought)** for a long time.
7. It was a particularly beautiful **(a. reef   b. wreath)**.
8. Where did they find that purple **(a. feather   b. heather)**?
9. There must be a **(a. bath   b. bat)** in that room.
10. She should have had a **(a. seat   b. sheet)**.
11. What are the **(a. prices   b. prizes)**?
12. Did you notice their **(a. ice   b. eyes)**?

B. Work with a partner. Take turns reading the sentences with one of the two words. Call out the letter of the word.

PRACTICE 10

A. Read the expressions in the language box and match them with their functions. Write **E** (expressing strong feelings politely), **D** (diffusing tension and refocusing), **S** (summarizing work accomplished), or **M** (making future plans).

B. You are taking part in a panel discussion at an international business conference. Work in small groups and discuss your opinions on the following topics:

> **Language for Discussion Management**
>
> _____ **a.** I'm sorry but I feel very strongly about . . .
> _____ **b.** Let's review what we've decided upon so far.
> _____ **c.** Let's take another look at our objectives.
> _____ **d.** We have only fifteen minutes left to discuss . . .
> _____ **e.** I can see the value in . . . but . . .
> _____ **f.** Wrapping up, we've . . .
> _____ **g.** Our next topic of discussion will be . . .
> _____ **h.** I really must disagree with . . .

- Making changes to adjust to other cultures versus doing things your way
- Spending money on cross-cultural communications training courses for the employees of international business corporations
- How to deal with gender differences in communication styles

Remember to follow these steps:

1. Express strong feelings politely.
2. Diffuse tensions and refocus when necessary.
3. Summarize work accomplished.
4. Make future plans.

Choose a topic from the box on which to write a thirty-minute timed essay. Give yourself five to ten minutes at the beginning to brainstorm your ideas and to plan your essay. Fill in your information below. Leave five minutes at the end to check your essay for errors.

TOPIC: _____

_____

IDEAS: _____

Topics

- Is it possible to change one's nonverbal communication style? Discuss why one would want to and how it could be done.
- Discuss the differences between telephone communication and face-to-face communication.
- What do people's conversational and nonverbal communication styles say about their personalities?
- How do humans and nonhuman animals communicate nonverbally together?

PLAN: _____

YOU'RE IN CHARGE!

UNIT FOUR OBJECTIVES: How well did you meet the objectives for this unit? Check the box next to each objective you feel you mastered.

GRAMMAR
❑ Passive modals in different tenses
❑ Multiple meanings of modals

LISTENING
❑ Listening for expressions of contrast or concession

SPEAKING
Reviewing discussion skills (4):
❑ Managing conflict
❑ Closing a discussion

PRONUNCIATION
❑ Consonant contrasts

READING
❑ Personalizing new information

WRITING
❑ Writing under time pressure
❑ Planning
❑ Editing

LEARNING STRATEGIES: Reflect on your use of learning strategies and thinking skills in this unit. What are some of the strategies you employed? Which ones were most successful for you?

Write your thoughts here.

_____

_____

_____

_____

_____

_____

_____

_____

_____

Unit 4 Learning Strategies
• Using context to determine meaning
• Making deductions
• Summarizing
• Taking notes
• Using prior knowledge
• Working cooperatively
• Brainstorming
• Using graphic organizers

PRACTICE 1

Ichiro has broken his arm and leg and is very unhappy about it. Work with a partner and brainstorm five inventions that already exist or that you can create to help Ichiro with his daily life.

Example: A wheelchair would help him move around.

1. _____

2. _____

3. _____

4. _____

5. _____

PRACTICE 2

Unscramble the vocabulary words. Then complete the sentences about inventions or inventors. Refer to page 56 in your student book for help.

a. syorg _____

b. pehy _____

c. deeg-tuntgci _____

d. enuvlide _____

e. toomnoclio _____

f. peorreshow _____

1. The news media can throw news of a new invention way out of proportion with all its _____ and hoopla.

2. A 12-_____ water-cooled engine was all that the Wright brothers used to power their first successful airplane.

3. Schools that are using _____ technology are preparing their students for the future.

4. Jacques Cousteau _____ his new invention, the Aqua-Lung,™ in 1943.

(continued on next page)

5. John Fitch first demonstrated the use of steam for water _____ in the late 1700s. Robert Fulton used that idea for the first steamboat in 1807.

6. The old-fashioned spinning _____ in movie camera mounts make more noise than the new ones.

PRACTICE 3

A. Two friends are playing a guessing game about inventions that they use in their daily lives. Work with a partner. Complete the conversation.

ROLES	CONVERSATION	FUNCTIONS
Sonia:	I'm thinking of something that I use outside.	Describe an invention.
Nadia:	Do you use it when you're cold?	Make a guess (or ask for another clue).
Sonia:	No, I don't. I use it to go places.	Give another clue.
Nadia:	That still could be lots of different things. Does it have _____?	Make a guess (or ask for another clue).
Sonia:	No, it has two wheels and handlebars.	Confirm the guess (or give another clue).
Nadia:	Is it a bicycle?	Make a guess.
Sonia:	Yes, _____.	Confirm the guess.

B. Take turns being the two friends and play a guessing game about inventions in your daily lives. Use the categories below.

a. transportation

b. cooking

c. around the house

d. technology

e. (your own idea)

PRACTICE 4

A. Complete this letter with *whose*, *which*, or *that*.

Inventors Unlimited
679 State Steet
Suite 452
Kansas City, MO 54677

Dear Potential Inventor:

You say you've got an idea for an invention **(1.)** _____ time has come?
You've been telling all your friends that this is the big one? Now you're wondering
how to take this invention from its idea stage to the marketplace,
(2.) _____ is the only way you are going to make any money from it. The
first question **(3.)** _____ you should be asking yourself is how you determine
if your idea is any good. Next, you should be wondering exactly how you are going
to benefit from your invention, **(4.)** _____ usefulness you are sure will be
recognized worldwide. You also need to know how you can protect your idea from
being stolen, **(5.)** _____ unfortunately happens all the time. Ideas
(6.) _____ are really good are stolen by people **(7.)** _____ skills are
limited to knowing how to take other people's ideas to market.

So, where can you find the answers to these questions? An inventors' conference
is the place for you. Inventors' conferences, **(8.)** _____ happen at various
times during the year, are very useful for showing "wannabe" inventors how to get
through the difficult process of transforming their brilliant ideas into financially
successful products, **(9.)** _____ is just what you need to do. At an inventors'
conference, you will meet inventors **(10.)** _____ creations you use every
day. Inventors, **(11.)** _____ creations have netted them a fortune, will be on
hand to help you navigate through the complicated process of getting a patent and
getting your invention manufactured and sold.

Attendance is limited, so register in advance to save up to $50.00.

B. Compare your answers with a partner's and explain your choices.

PRACTICE 5

Combine the sentences to make new sentences using *whose* or *which*. Write your new sentences on the lines. Then compare your answers with a partner's.

1. Some inventions were invented very recently. These inventions are useful and entertaining.

   _____

2. For example, CDs were only invented in the 1980s. The name CD means compact disc.

   _____

3. Now long-playing (LP) records are obsolete. That's OK with me since CDs have better sound quality.

   _____

4. The next generation will undoubtedly see more innovations in music recording. The next generation's would-be inventors are still in school.

   _____

PRACTICE 6

Complete the following sentences with *whose*, *which*, or *that*. Add any commas necessary. Then compare your answers with a partner's.

1. If it weren't for George Washington Carver _____

   _____

2. Many inventors are thought to be visionaries _____

   _____

3. Some inventions have no known inventor _____

   _____

4. Toothpaste was invented about 5,000 years ago _____

   _____

5. Canned food was invented in the early 1800s by the British _____

   _____

6. It wasn't until the 1860s that the can opener was invented _____

   _____

A. Reduce the relative clauses to phrases in the following sentences by crossing out any extra words. Add commas as necessary. Write **NC** (No Change) next to those sentences that cannot be reduced.

Example: Chocolate Chip cookies, ~~which are~~ well loved by children, were invented by mistake.

_____ **1.** This fortunate mistake happened when a woman named Ruth Wakefield had to substitute broken bits of a chocolate bar for the unsweetened chocolate she had run out of.

_____ **2.** The unsweetened chocolate that was used by Ruth for baking chocolate cookies melted and was absorbed by the flour.

_____ **3.** However, when the cookies with the broken bits of chocolate were baking Ruth discovered that the chocolate bits that she used didn't melt in the same way.

_____ **4.** The children who were visiting were delighted with her new creation.

_____ **5.** Potato chips which are now the number one snack food in America were another fortunate creative mistake.

_____ **6.** In 1853, a chef who was named George Crum had a customer return a plate of French fries complaining that they were not cooked enough or sliced thinly enough.

_____ **7.** George who was getting angry sliced the potatoes paper thin and fried them until they were crisp.

_____ **8.** Crum's potato chips were an instant hit.

B. Compare your answers with a partner's and explain your choices.

PRACTICE 8

A. Before You Listen Discuss with a partner. Have you ever thought of inventing something to make life easier or more fun? If you had the time and money, what would you invent?

B. Listen to some friends talk about a modern invention. Number the statements in the order in which they occurred.

_____ **a.** Southern Californian Plastics Company manufactured the original flying plastic disc for Mr. Morrison.

_____ **b.** William Morrison patented his plastic flying disc in 1958.

_____ **c.** Yale University students tossed around Frisbie Baking Company's pie tins.

_____ **d.** The Greeks used a flying disc in the Olympic Games.

_____ **e.** The flying disc was given the name Frisbee®.

_____ **f.** Wham-O Company bought the flying disc design rights from William Morrison.

playing with a flying disc

C. Work with a partner and compare your answers to Part B. Then discuss the following questions.

1. What was Kenji studying for?
2. Who was going to help Kenji study?
3. What did the Frisbie Baking Company have to do with Frisbees®?
4. What did Kenji say he would like to be lucky about?
5. Is the Frisbee® a good invention? Why or why not?

PRACTICE 9

A. Predict the stress and intonation patterns of the conversation. Underline all the stressed syllables. After each question, draw a rising arrow (↗) or a falling arrow (↘) to indicate the intonation.

NANCY: OK, Kenji. Here's your next question. Who invented the automatic traffic signal?

KENJI: Oh, that's easy. It was Garrett A. Morgan, wasn't it?

NANCY: That's great. Can you tell me the year?

KENJI: Was it 1924?

NANCY: No, I'm sorry, Kenji. It was 1923. What else did Mr. Morgan invent?

KENJI: I believe he invented the first gas mask, didn't he?

NANCY: Yes, that's right. It was called the Morgan safety hood, and it was used to rescue 32 men trapped during an underground explosion. People were very impressed.

KENJI: Yes, I know. Mr. Morgan was an African American businessman and inventor who developed many useful products.

B. Listen to the conversation to check your predictions.

C. Work with a partner and take turns reading the conversation aloud.

PRACTICE 10

A. You are taking part in an international symposium on recent discoveries in your field. Plan a two- to three-minute presentation on your latest discovery. Use one of the following topics:

- Invent an important discovery in the area of your choice.

- Think of a discovery or invention you are familiar with and present it as if it were your own.

- (Your own idea)

B. Work in small groups. Deliver your presentation using the notes you developed in Part A.

> **Remember to:**
> 1. Introduce the topic with a preview statement that expresses your purpose and main idea.
> 2. Support your topic with two or three points.
> 3. Have a conclusion to your presentation.
> 4. Use simple vocabulary and structures.
> 5. Have explicit transitions.
> 6. Keep the interest and knowledge of your audience in mind.

PRACTICE 11

A. Reread the essay on pages 63–65 in your student book about the history of the pencil. Work with a partner. Identify the parts of a research paper that may be found in the article and cite examples.

——— **a.** thesis statement   ——— **d.** examples

——— **b.** supporting argument   ——— **e.** reference to a source

——— **c.** background information   ——— **f.** summarizing statement

YOU'RE IN CHARGE!

UNIT FIVE OBJECTIVES: How well did you meet the objectives for this unit? Check the box next to each objective you feel you mastered.

GRAMMAR

❑ Relative clauses: *whose/which/that*

❑ Using identifying and non-identifying relative clauses

❑ Reducing relative clauses to phrases

LISTENING

❑ Listening for sequence of events and inference

SPEAKING

❑ Focusing on the components of an oral presentation

PRONUNCIATION

❑ Word stress and intonation

READING

❑ Distinguishing between facts and commentary

WRITING

❑ Analyzing a research paper

LEARNING STRATEGIES: Reflect on your use of learning strategies and thinking skills in this unit. What are some of the strategies you employed? Which ones were most successful for you?

Write your thoughts here.

_____

_____

_____

_____

_____

_____

_____

_____

_____

Unit 5 Learning Strategies

- Using context to determine meaning
- Making inferences
- Using prior knowledge
- Skimming
- Working cooperatively
- Making predictions
- Analyzing

HOOKED ON HORROR

Almost every culture has a "bogey man," a person or creature who will "come and get you" if you don't behave. In Germany, the "bogey man" is known as *schreckbild*, and in many Latin American countries as *El Coco*. Ask your classmates what fearful creatures they were warned about as children.

Complete the crossword puzzle. Refer to page 68 in your student book for help.

ACROSS

5. believable
6. someone who commits a crime

DOWN

1. deceived
2. very upsetting to see or hear about
3. unharmed
4. to succeed in finding something

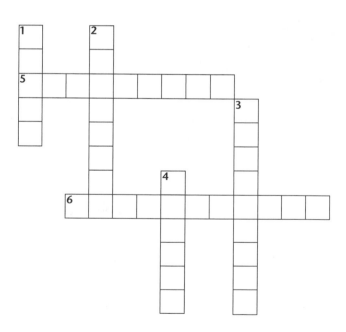

PRACTICE 3

A. Two horror fan club members are discussing possible topics for their meetings next year. Work with a partner. Complete the conversation.

ROLES	CONVERSATION	FUNCTIONS
Ben:	Let's invite a film director to our next meeting who can explain some of the tricks they use for special effects.	Make a suggestion.
Amalia:	I think a director would be difficult to get, but I know a makeup artist who _____.	Reject the suggestion, and make an alternative suggestion.
Ben:	That's a good idea and we could _____ _____.	Respond to the suggestion, and make another suggestion.

B. Take turns being the fan club members and discuss these possible meeting topics.

    a. showing a horror movie

    b. inviting a horror memorabilia collector

    c. visiting a horror museum

    d. inviting a horror story writer

    e. (your own idea)

PRACTICE 4

Write sentences using the cues and the verbs in parentheses. Add additional words as necessary.

    Example: mad scientist/victim   (make/drink)
        <u>The mad scientist made the victim drink the potion.</u>

    1. doctor/patient (make/take)

    _____

    2. teacher/student (have/memorize)

    _____

    3. director/actor (get/repeat)

    _____

    4. grandparents/children (let/eat)

    _____

A. Combine the sentences using the expressions from the box. Write your new sentences on the lines, making any necessary changes.

> as   as a result of   so   due to   in that   consequently   since

a computer animator at work

1. Today's horror movies are more graphic than ever before. Imaging technology has grown in sophistication.

_____

_____

2. Visual images can be adjusted pixel by pixel on computers. Extraordinary special effects can be created.

_____

_____

3. Today, it is common to see heads turn full circle and hands crawl across the floor on the screen. Techniques in computer simulation have improved.

_____

_____

4. The body and movements of a "real" actor can be scanned into a computer. It is possible to build a visually convincing monster or alien around the actor's form.

_____

_____

5. Horror fans now expect more spectacular scenes. It is difficult for writers to come up with new, shocking, and gruesome effects.

_____

_____

B. Compare your answers with a partner's and explain your choices.

PRACTICE 6

Use the cues to write sentences with *so* + adjective + *that* or *such* + noun phrase + *that*. Share your sentences with a partner.

Examples: I am angry.
<u>I am so angry that I could explode!</u>

It was a good party.
<u>It was such a good party that no one wanted to leave!</u>

1. It is an expensive computer.

_____

2. The experience was terrifying.

_____

3. She was embarrassed.

_____

4. It was a disturbing special effect.

_____

5. He is a horror movie fan.

_____

PRACTICE 7

Circle the phrases that best complete this story about La Llorona. Compare your answers with a partner's.

No one really knows where the legend of La Llorona comes from, **(1. so as/so)** this woman remains a mystery and a misery. But ask a person from Latin America, the southwestern United States, or Spain if they ever heard of La Llorona and they will tell you they heard about her from their parents. As children, they were told to come in the house by dark **(2. so that/so as)** to escape La Llorona, who grabs children on the loose. Wandering near a river is especially dangerous. There are many versions of the legend of this sad woman, **(3. in order that/so that)** you might hear of her as a jealous, vengeful woman or a sweet, innocent maiden.

In most of the stories, La Llorona is betrayed or deserted by her "man." **(4. In order to/So that)** relieve her grief or to avenge the man she trusted, she drowns or kills her children. After realizing what she has done, she kills herself. Over the years, people have reported seeing a woman dressed in white roaming near rivers and crying loudly **(5. in order to/so that)** let everyone hear her sorrow. For parents, La Llorona works as an effective scare tactic **(6. in order to/so that)** keep children close to home.

PRACTICE 8

A. Before You Listen Discuss with a partner whether you think the horror genre is best represented in books or movies. Give your reasons. Name your favorite horror story. Was it ever made into a movie?

B. Listen to an excerpt from a radio show on writing. Take notes on the items below. Then compare your notes with a partner's.

1. Topic of today's show: _____

2. Title of the writer's latest biography: _____

3. Influences on Barbara Grant and her choice of subject: _____
   _____
   _____
   _____

4. Three examples of Stephen King's work: _____
   _____
   _____

5. How reading tales of horror might help readers: _____
   _____
   _____

C. Discuss these questions in small groups.

- Have you ever read a story or novel by Stephen King? If so, which one(s)?
- Have you ever seen a movie based on one of his works?
- Do you think that tales of violence and horror are helpful or harmful?

PRACTICE 9

A. Predict which sounds will be reduced and held in each sentence by underlining them. Some sentences contain more than one pair.

1. One kind of horror movie is the vivid disaster film.

2. Disaster movies such as *The Towering Inferno* and *Earthquake* captivated and delighted filmgoers in the early 1970s.

(continued on next page)

3. The catastrophe at the center of such movies was always shown in gruesome, horrid detail.

4. The disaster revealed both the worst and best in human nature.

5. The object of the disaster was always one of humankind's proudest technological achievements—an unsinkable ocean liner, a fireproof skyscraper, or a jumbo jet.

B. Listen to the sentences to check your predictions.

C. Work with a partner and take turns saying the sentences.

PRACTICE 10

A. Work in small groups. Choose one of the topics below and imagine you are preparing a presentation. Each group member should think of one attention-getting opener for the topic and share it with the group.

- Cultural variations in horror films
- The origin of a holiday for the dead
- Advances in special effects
- Urban legends
- Controlling fear
- (Your own idea)

INTRODUCTION
Write your opener here.

_____

_____

_____

_____

_____

B. Use the same topic to develop an effective conclusion in which you restate the main idea and offer a memorable ending. Share it with your group.

CONCLUSION
Write your memorable ending here.

_____

_____

_____

_____

_____

A.   Imagine you have chosen the general topic of films as a subject for a paper. Narrow the topic and write it on the line.

_____

B.   Complete an idea map on a separate sheet of paper, noting down some areas you might explore concerning your topic.

Example:

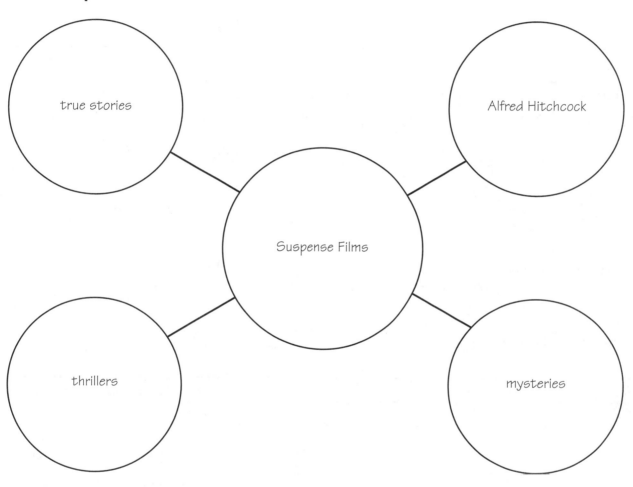

C.   What will be your position or viewpoint on your narrowed topic? Write a possible thesis statement on the lines.

_____

_____

_____

D.   Develop an outline for your paper and exchange it with a partner. Comment on your partner's work and receive feedback on yours.

YOU'RE IN CHARGE!

Unit Six Objectives: How well did you meet the objectives for this unit? Check the box next to each objective you feel you mastered.

GRAMMAR
- ❑ Causatives: *have, let, make,* and *get*
- ❑ Expressions of cause and effect
- ❑ Expressions of purpose

LISTENING
- ❑ Listening for supporting arguments

SPEAKING
- ❑ Making effective introductions

PRONUNCIATION
- ❑ Reducing and holding sounds

READING
- ❑ Recognizing tone and level of formality

WRITING
- ❑ Choosing and narrowing a topic

Learning Strategies: Reflect on your use of learning strategies and thinking skills in this unit. What are some of the strategies you employed? Which ones were most successful for you?

Write your thoughts here.

Unit 6 Learning Strategies
- Using prior knowledge
- Using context to determine meaning
- Identifying cause-and-effect relationships
- Brainstorming
- Taking notes
- Making predictions
- Using graphic organizers

PRACTICE 1

Who or what helps you to decide on a career? On a scale of **1** (highly important) to **5** (not important), rate each of these factors that might influence you in making a career decision. Share your ratings in small groups. What similarities and differences are there in your group?

—— **a.** older relatives

—— **b.** brothers or sisters

—— **c.** teachers

—— **d.** friends

—— **e.** parents' friends

—— **f.** career counselor

—— **g.** career tests

—— **h.** books on different occupations

—— **i.** information from the Internet

—— **j.** (your own idea)

PRACTICE 2

Use the words or expressions in the box to complete the conversation. Refer to page 84 in your student book for help.

JAMAL: Did you meet with your school adviser yet, Li-Ping?

LI-PING: I'm going to see her tomorrow and she said not to **(1.)** _____ anything like choosing a major until she's given me one of those aptitude or skill inventories.

JAMAL: What do you mean by "aptitude"?

LI-PING: That's your natural ability or skill for something. Like I might make a great business manager and even **(2.)** _____ someday because I love business.

JAMAL: You, Li-Ping, love business? I'm trying to **(3.)** _____ here, but I've seen you give the wrong change when we worked in the bookstore last year. Have you been **(4.)** _____ I didn't know about?

LI-PING: You see, you don't know everything, Jamal. You **(5.)** _____ jumping to conclusions. Remember when you said that Melvin's parents **(6.)** _____ to take over their business?

JAMAL: Yeah, that's what I thought. I didn't know they just wanted him to get a job, any job.

> keep an open mind
> have a knack for
> were after him
> jump into
> run the company
> nursing an ambition

PRACTICE 3

A. An employee is asking her boss for advice about her future in the company. Work with a partner. Complete the conversation.

ROLES	CONVERSATION	FUNCTIONS
Employee:	I really love working here, but I'd like to have more responsibility and to learn new skills. Do you think I should go back to school or apply for more training here?	State a problem.
Boss:	Those are both good possibilities for getting ahead. It's important that _____ _____.	Advise someone of what is important or essential.
Employee:	So what do you think I should do?	Ask for further advice.
Boss:	I suggest that _____ _____ _____.	Give a recommendation.

B. Take turns being the employee and the boss and discuss these other possibilities.

   a. work part-time or full-time
   b. take a leave of absence from work or stay in the job
   c. change to a different department or stay in the same department
   d. work the night shift or work during the day
   e. (your own idea)

PRACTICE 4

A. Two friends are talking about how to find career information. Complete the sentences by circling the correct forms of the verbs in parentheses.

MAYA: I'm stuck, Eric. Maybe you can help me out. My boyfriend's father is demanding that my boyfriend **(1. takes over/take over)** the business, but Greg **(2. not want/doesn't want)** to. He's more interested in physical therapy.

ERIC: Well, I suggest that he **(3. talks/talk)** to his father then. Don't you think it's important that his father **(4. understands/understand)** why he **(5. wants/want)** to study instead of work in the business?

MAYA: Well, of course, but it's vital that we **(6. get/not get)** some data.

ERIC: You mean information about whether physical therapy **(7. is/be)** a growing field?

MAYA: Yeah, something like that.

ERIC: Well, I suggest that your boyfriend **(8. looks/look)** on the Internet. There **(9. be/are)** lots of websites with career information. And let's **(10. not forget/forget)** the professional associations for physical therapists. They can help too.

MAYA: Wow, thanks so much, Eric. This is great advice!

B. Compare your answers with a partner's. Discuss what you would recommend for Maya and her boyfriend.

PRACTICE 5

Read this letter from an employment counselor and correct the six mistakes in verb forms. The first one is done for you.

Dear Mr. Chen:

Thank you for your letter asking for advice about how to get

a job in Los Angeles. I suggest that you ~~looks~~ *look* on the Internet under

"newspapers" and finds the newspapers in Los Angeles. It is

essential that the newspaper be current. I advise you not have read

an old newspaper because those jobs can already taken. It's also

important that you will look for websites where you can post your

résumé or respond to ads for jobs.

Finally, contact the local business association and see what they

are recommending.

Good luck in your job search.

Sincerely,

Martin Soler

PRACTICE 6

A. Give advice to each of the following people by completing the sentences.

a visit to a Career Day fair

1. Susanna wants to become an accountant but she doesn't have enough money to enroll in a university.

   I recommend that _____.

2. Victor can't decide whether to go to the university after high school or take a few years off to work and travel.

   It's important that _____.

3. Abdul's parents are pressuring him to follow in his father's footsteps and become a barber.

   I suggest that _____.

4. Diana is twenty-five years old and still can't decide what she wants to do with her life.

   It is vital that _____.

5. Jobs in Taro's field have suddenly dried up. He doesn't know what to do.

   I recommend that _____.

6. Marta is halfway through her course of study at the university but isn't interested in becoming a doctor anymore.

   I suggest that Marta not _____.

7. Mei-Li is looking for a study abroad program where she can spend the next semester.

   It is essential that _____.

8. After graduating from a university, Steven was offered one job in Bogotá and another job in Miami. He doesn't know which one to choose.

   I advise that _____.

B. In small groups, discuss the advice you gave. How similar or different were your recommendations?

PRACTICE 7

A. **Before You Listen** Discuss with a partner. What sources do you use to get information? Which sources do you think are most reliable?

B. Listen to the first part of a conversation between a husband and wife. Then answer the questions.

1. What's the topic of their conversation?

_____

2. Who is puzzled?

_____

3. Why is that person puzzled?

_____

4. Where is the person going to look for information?

_____

C. Listen to the second part of the conversation. Why is the person still puzzled?

_____

D. Compare your answers with a partner's.

PRACTICE 8

A. Predict the pronunciation of the vowel sounds. Match the words in Column B with the words in Column A that have the same vowel sounds. Write the letter on the blank line.

COLUMN A	COLUMN B
_____ **1.** hot	**a.** through
_____ **2.** drew	**b.** end
_____ **3.** help	**c.** keep
_____ **4.** friends	**d.** career
_____ **5.** school	**e.** level
_____ **6.** real	**f.** shoe

B. Listen to the words to check your predictions.

C. Work with a partner and take turns reading the words.

PRACTICE 9

A. Your teacher has asked you to give a five-minute presentation to the class about a specific career. Work in small groups. Use the following steps to plan your presentation. Make notes in the chart.

1. Decide which career you will present.

2. Decide what visual aids will help; consider classroom resources. (For example, flip charts, slides, transparencies, computer, chalkboard, or handouts)

3. Make an outline of the presentation.

Example: Career: Nursing

Visual Aids: Flip chart and slides

using visual aids

Notes
Career:
Visual Aids:
Outline:

B. Work with another group and give your presentation to them.

PRACTICE 10

The following excerpts are from the unit reading on pages 89–91 in your student book. Work with a partner to paraphrase each excerpt on the lines below. Join with another pair and check the accuracy of the paraphrased excerpts.

1. "I spent a lot of time alone in bed, staring at the ceiling, imagining possible lives. My present existence—scraping through classes, getting in fights, partying with the guys, sitting at the dinner table with my mother, swallowing forkfuls of silence—filled me with dissatisfaction. There was no direction to it, no intensity. No *power*."

   <u>The author felt that the way he was living his life had no meaning and he was very</u>

   <u>dissatisfied.</u>
   _____

   _____

2. "My days took on a silent, submarine quality as I prepared myself for my future. People receded from me, and I let them go gladly. The friends who scoffed or tried to incite me to fight, the teachers who discussed me in amazed whispers in the staff lounge, even my mother who watched me thankfully but without understanding. They were merely distractions, ripples on a distant surface which had little to do with my life. I would feel the same way about my classmates in college."

   _____

   _____

   _____

   _____

3. "When I made my first million, I sent my mother a check for a hundred thousand dollars. It was the first time I'd corresponded with her since I left home. Oh she'd write to me, not often but regularly, telling me what she was doing. . . . After a while the letters would come and I'd leave them unopened. Sometimes they'd get misplaced before I read them. I never wrote back."

   _____

   _____

   _____

   _____

YOU'RE IN CHARGE!

UNIT SEVEN OBJECTIVES: How well did you meet the objectives for this unit? Check the box next to each objective you feel you mastered.

GRAMMAR	**LISTENING**	**SPEAKING**
❏ The subjunctive in noun clauses	❏ Listening for excerpts and summaries	❏ Using visual aids

PRONUNCIATION	**READING**	**WRITING**
❏ Different spellings of the same vowel sounds	❏ Understanding use of quotation marks in reading conversations	❏ Citing the source of a quote or idea ❏ Paraphrasing the ideas of others

LEARNING STRATEGIES: Reflect on your use of learning strategies and thinking skills in this unit. What are some of the strategies you employed? Which ones were most successful for you?

Write your thoughts here.

_____

_____

_____

_____

_____

_____

_____

_____

_____

Unit 7 Learning Strategies

- Using prior knowledge
- Using context to determine meaning
- Categorizing
- Comparing and contrasting
- Paraphrasing
- Using graphic organizers
- Summarizing key ideas
- Working cooperatively

PRACTICE 1

Imagine that we had fourteen-hour days instead of twenty-four-hour days. Work with a partner to brainstorm a list of ways that our lives would be affected by this change.

PRACTICE 2

Match the definitions from the box with the italicized words in the sentences. Refer to page 96 in your student book for help.

_____ **1.** Hector used to be on the night *shift* from 12 midnight to 8 A.M., but it was too difficult for him to sleep when he got home.

_____ **2.** I heard that the research institute was adding a *chronobiologist* to their team.

_____ **3.** The sailboat captain stayed awake all night to prevent his boat from *drifting* into the underwater reefs.

_____ **4.** If you take a midnight walk, you will see the *nocturnal* creatures that begin their day at sunset.

_____ **5.** The *volunteers* for the sleep experiment were awakened every two hours.

_____ **6.** Passing in and out of REM periods as we sleep is an example of an *ultradian* cycle.

_____ **7.** Global warming, El Niño, and earthquakes are all *geophysical* events.

_____ **8.** Humans seem to function naturally on a *circadian* cycle, even when they are deprived of external cues.

_____ **9.** While there are suggested cures for jet lag, researchers would like to *ascertain* which is the most effective.

_____ **10.** During a flight from Montreal to China, I *reset* my watch three or four times.

a. people who agree to perform a service

b. to find out with certainty

c. varying from a set direction

d. active at night

e. to change the setting or reading

f. relating to the physical processes and phenomena of the earth

g. having approximately 24-hour periods or cycles

h. someone who studies biological rhythms

i. a scheduled period of work or duty

j. cycles or periods less than 24-hours long

A. A doctor is asking a patient about her work schedule to determine the cause of her feeling tired. Work with a partner. Complete the conversation.

ROLES	CONVERSATION	FUNCTIONS
Doctor:	Do you work a lot of hours?	Ask about general problems.
Patient:	_____ _____	Answer the question and provide details.
Doctor:	Are you required to work overtime?	Ask a follow-up question.
Patient:	_____ _____	Respond and elaborate.

B. Take turns being the doctor and the patient. Ask and answer questions about the following complaints.

 a. blurry vision   **d.** frequent headaches

 b. difficulty sleeping   **e.** (your own idea)

 c. lack of appetite

Complete the passage with the correct form of the verbs in parentheses.

  Some of us would like **(1. know)** _____ more about the best time of day for people **(2. take)** _____ medicine, exercise, or rest. According to a recent book, **(3. pay)** _____ attention to our body's symptoms and **(4. note)** _____ the time of day when they occur can be vital. Different illnesses seem **(5. peak)** _____ at different times of the day. For example, asthma sufferers report more attacks **(6. occur)** _____ during the night. At-risk cardiac patients are advised **(7. be)** _____ careful in the morning, when heart attacks and strokes are more likely **(8. occur)** _____. Migraine headaches, high blood pressure, and nasal allergies also seem **(9. strike)** _____ in the morning hours.

  In addition, **(10. take)** _____ certain medicine, such as aspirin, at a particular time of day can increase its effectiveness. So the next time you get a headache or a pain in your back, don't neglect **(11. write)** _____ down the time of day and start **(12. look)** _____ for patterns.

PRACTICE 5

A. Read this journal entry of a volunteer in a sleep experiment. Correct the twelve mistakes in verb forms. The first one is done for you.

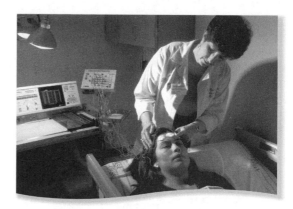

a sleep experiment volunteer

May 15

           I volunteered for this sleep experiment ~~to think~~ **thinking** that I would get extra credit for my psychology course. Now they're telling us not expecting a better grade in the course just for to do the experiment. There are five other students to stay here with me and I'm stuck in this laboratory sleeping for the next two days. When we arrived at the lab beginning the experiment, they attached wires connect to various parts of our bodies. The researchers have been waking us up several times doing exercises and playing games. Then we sleep again. Then we wake up and take turns eating and to shower. It's very disturbing waking up so often. We don't know what time it is. It would be easy telling if they hadn't hidden all the clocks. I'd like writing more but we have sleeping again.

Good night?

Sleep Subject #305

B. Compare your answers with a partner's and explain your choices.

PRACTICE 6

A. Rewrite the following sentences using a possessive adjective and a gerund.

Example: The doctor recommended that he get help for his sleeping disorder.

<u>The doctor recommended his getting help for his sleeping disorder.</u>

1. I appreciate that you bought my new book on nocturnal animals.

   _____

2. The research team didn't anticipate that they needed a chronobiologist.

   _____

3. Marcos liked that she was a night owl and slept late.

   _____

4. They remembered that she studied the circadian rhythms of rats and mice.

   _____

5. Kyoko recommends that you take the medicine at night before bedtime.

   _____

6. He appreciates that they get up early to go jogging.

   _____

7. The therapist recommended that she change her routine.

   _____

8. Do you remember that I felt jet lagged on our last trip?

   _____

B. Compare your answers with a partner's and explain your choices.

a hamster

PRACTICE 7

A. Before You Listen Discuss in small groups. How do you think biological clocks function in animals? Give examples. How do you think biological clocks function in plants? Give examples.

B. Listen to a question-and-answer session between an animal researcher and some students visiting his laboratory. Use the chart to note the questions and answers. Then compare your notes with a partner's and add any information that you missed.

Questions	Answers

C. Use your notes in the chart and what you remember from the listening to complete the sentences.

1. Hamsters are _____ and therefore more active at night.

2. A circadian rhythm in a living organism equals a period of approximately _____ hours.

3. The researchers were able to measure the hamster's active period at night by using a _____ to record the activity.

4. Endogenous rhythms do not depend on _____ cues, but on internal rhythms.

5. An example of an endogenous rhythm is when some animals _____ in cold weather.

PRACTICE 8

A.   Predict the pronunciation of the vowel sounds. Match the words in Column B with the words in Column A that have the same vowel sounds. Write the letter on the line.

COLUMN A	COLUMN B
_____ **1.** all	**a.** only
_____ **2.** how	**b.** blind
_____ **3.** day	**c.** safe
_____ **4.** goes	**d.** hours
_____ **5.** most	**e.** know
_____ **6.** why	**f.** fought

B.   Listen to the words to check your predictions.

C.   Work with a partner and take turns reading the words.

PRACTICE 9

A.   Read the following sentences about delivery techniques for presentations. Write **T** (true) or **F** (false).

_____ **1.** You'll make a better impression on your audience if you look and sound confident.

_____ **2.** Speak quickly so that you can say more in the amount of time you have to make your presentation.

_____ **3.** Use lots of gestures when you speak, especially twisting your hair or your clothes.

_____ **4.** In order to be heard by everyone, speak loudly and strongly enough for the size of the room.

_____ **5.** Try to look at everyone in the audience, making eye contact without staring in just one direction.

_____ **6.** Don't rehearse your talk or it won't sound natural when you face your audience.

B.   Work in small groups. Talk for one minute about an aspect of delivery that is most difficult for you. For example, if making eye contact is difficult for you, talk about why as you focus on moving your eyes around the audience.

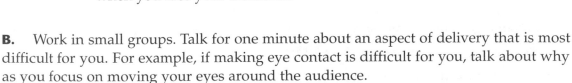

PRACTICE 10

A. Mark the following statements **T** (true) or **F** (false) according to the guidelines for citations that you read about on page 106 in your student book.

_____ **1.** A citation is placed in your paper at the end of the quote or paraphrase.

_____ **2.** A direct quote where the author's name is mentioned doesn't need a citation.

_____ **3.** A paraphrased quote never needs a citation.

_____ **4.** The information in a citation differs depending on whether it is a quote or a paraphrase.

_____ **5.** *Et al.* is used in a citation when there are multiple authors and their names have been mentioned before.

_____ **6.** If a work you are citing has two authors, you only need to mention one of them in your citation.

_____ **7.** It's not necessary to include the page number of the original work in your citation.

_____ **8.** A bibliography and a citation are basically the same thing.

B. Compare your answers with a partner's and discuss how to change the false statements to true ones.

C. A student who was preparing a paper about humans' biological clocks wrote the following bibliographical notes. Unfortunately, the student forgot important information in each source. Work with a partner and note on the line what type of information is missing, according to APA style.

Example: Lamberg, L., & Smolensky, M. (2000). *The body clock guide to better health: How to use your body's natural clock to fight illness and achieve maximum health. Henry Holt & Company. <u>Place of publication is missing.</u>*

1. Persaud, R. (January 10). It's a sad, sad world without the sun. *The Daily Telegraph* (London), pg. 26. _____

2. (2000, June 1). How a 24-hour lifestyle disrupts the body clock's natural settings. *The Scotsman*, pg. 6. _____

3. Moore-Ede, M.C., Sulzman, F.M., & Fuller, C.A. (1982). *The clocks that time us: physiology of the circadian timing system.* Cambridge, Mass.

_____

YOU'RE IN CHARGE!

UNIT EIGHT OBJECTIVES: How well did you meet the objectives for this unit? Check the box next to each objective you feel you mastered.

GRAMMAR
- ❑ Gerunds and infinitives

LISTENING
- ❑ Listening to take question-and-answer notes

SPEAKING
- ❑ Using effective delivery techniques

PRONUNCIATION
- ❑ Different spellings of the same vowel sounds

READING
- ❑ Reading for credibility of author's sources and examples

WRITING
- ❑ Creating a bibliography and gathering information
- ❑ Citing sources

LEARNING STRATEGIES: Reflect on your use of learning strategies and thinking skills in this unit. What are some of the strategies you employed? Which ones were most successful for you?

Write your thoughts here.

_____

_____

_____

_____

_____

_____

_____

_____

Unit 8 Learning Strategies

- Using context to determine meaning
- Taking notes
- Categorizing
- Making predictions
- Paraphrasing
- Using graphic organizers
- Working cooperatively

PRACTICE 1

In addition to volcanoes, other natural occurrences have played a role in shaping our planet. Work with a partner and take turns describing how the following phenomena have helped to shape the way our earth looks today.

- water (rivers, oceans, lakes, etc.)

- earth movements (earthquakes, landslides, etc.)

- glaciation (glaciers, icebergs, etc.)

PRACTICE 2

Complete the crossword puzzle. Refer to page 109 in your student book for help.

ACROSS

2. traditional customs and stories
3. a feeling of extreme anger
4. the round open top of a volcano
5. changing feelings

DOWN

1. began a new village or town
2. stopped fighting with no clear winner

A. A student is asking a librarian about a recent event in the news. Work with a partner. Complete the conversation.

Roles	Conversation	Functions
Student:	Did you hear about that recent earthquake in Central America?	Ask about a natural phenomenon.
Librarian:	Yes, it was a real tragedy.	Describe the event.
Student:	What happened? I didn't have a chance to follow the story.	Ask for information.
Librarian:	_____ _____ .	Provide details.
Student:	Hmmm . . . I didn't know that.	Encourage the speaker to continue.
Librarian:	_____ _____ .	Elaborate on the story.

B. Take turns being the student and the librarian. Ask and answer questions about these other events in the news.

- **a.** a wildfire
- **b.** a national election
- **c.** an explosion
- **d.** (your own idea)

PRACTICE 4

Classify the parts of a noun phrase from the box by writing them in their appropriate category on the chart. Compare your answers with a partner's.

Parts of a Noun Phrase

several	his	half of	extremely	very
a	the	red	huge	mostly
every	European	cold	silk	that

Pre-determiners	Determiners	Quantifiers	Intensifiers	Adjectives

PRACTICE 5

A. Unscramble the following sentences and rewrite them on the lines.

1. The active located still Arenal Volcano
is in Costa Rica northwestern.

Arenal Volcano, Costa Rica

_____

2. In 1968, after an dramatically active intensely 10-hour period, it erupted seismic.

_____

3. The molten lava hot extremely and gases 78 people killed and destroyed toxic
12 square kilometers of land.

_____

4. Today, this ash, gases, and lava stratovolcano 1657-meter still spouts restless.

_____

5. curious journey to the town near Many Arenal Volcano visitors foreign
to catch a glimpse of its magnificence.

_____

6. However, the foggy the top of the volcano very weather makes it impossible
to see on most days.

_____

B. Compare your answers with a partner's and explain your choices.

PRACTICE 6

Read this travel brochure and correct the ten mistakes in word order in the
noun phrases. The first two are done for you.

>   _extremely_   _most_
> Looking for an ^ exciting ~~extremely~~ vacation? Then call the ^ trusted ~~most~~
> name in travel adventure—The Thrill of a Lifetime Vacation Club!
>
> That's right. You'll get a thrill of a vacation lifetime for a customer first-time price.
> Picture yourself! You'll bike the curvy mountain cool roads of western Canada on
> our mountain state-of-the-art bikes. If you enjoy sparkling warm blue clear water,
> we'll take you to distant exotic Bali where you can raft down the exciting fun-filled
> fast rapids. Our travel-experienced consultants are waiting to hear from you.
> Call (888) 456-0002.

PRACTICE 7

A. Work with a partner and choose words from the box to make descriptive sentences about the following places or things. Add additional words as necessary to complete the sentences.

Example: chair

The comfortable antique green leather chair
was the best birthday gift I received.

leather	most
antique	elegant
comfortable	beautiful
black	cheap
woolen	small
warm	rectangular
new	silk
large	metal
expensive	green
few	red
several	one
of	a
the	

1. scarf

_____

_____

2. hotel

_____

_____

3. apartment

_____

_____

4. cars

_____

_____

5. coat

_____

_____

6. flowers

_____

_____

7. clock

_____

_____

8. computers

_____

_____

B. Make a list of five additional places or things. Work with a partner. Take turns describing one thing on your list without telling your partner what it is. Have your partner guess the place or thing you are describing.

PRACTICE 8

A. Before You Listen Discuss with a partner what steps you would take in an emergency situation. How would you let your family know that you are safe?

B. Listen to a panel of experts discuss emergency preparedness. After you listen, answer the questions. Then compare your answers with a partner's.

1. What is a signal flare?

   _____

2. What is a meeting plan?

   _____

3. What fears do children have after a disaster?

   _____

   _____

4. How can we help children cope with their fears?

   _____

   _____

C. Work with a partner. Make a list of specific items for the disaster supply kit and share your list with the class.

Food	Clothes	Tools	Special Supplies
			battery-powered radio

PRACTICE 9

A. Predict the division of the sentences in the following paragraph into thought groups. Divide the thought groups with slashes (/).

When a natural disaster occurs, the surviving victims may develop what is called Post-Traumatic Stress Disorder (PTSD). This disorder has been well documented, and researchers have drawn up a list of symptoms that might appear over time. Some survivors develop immediate reactions—shock and denial—which are later replaced by irritability, depression, nightmares, dissociation, anxiety, and physical symptoms such as headaches or nausea. Other survivors do not have immediate reactions, but take a few months or longer to develop the same symptoms. It's important to seek professional help if the signs of traumatic stress do not lessen in severity.

B. Listen to the paragraph to check your predictions.

C. Work with a partner and take turns reading the passage aloud.

PRACTICE 10

You are part of an environmental organization and have been asked to give an informative talk to a group of students. Work in small groups to discuss an environmental issue that can be described as a process. First decide on the specialized vocabulary that is involved. Then take turns talking about this issue, explaining the process involved. Use words such as *first*, *next*, *then*, and *finally* to help you.

Example: deforestation

Specialized Vocabulary: clearcutting, logging, forest conservation, old-growth forests

Eucalyptus trees being logged

PRACTICE 11

Use the same environmental issue that you discussed in Practice 10 to develop a written essay. First complete the chart in preparation for writing. Remember to use transition sentences to end your support paragraphs when you write your full essay.

ENVIRONMENTAL ISSUE:
SPECIALIZED VOCABULARY:
OUTLINE:

YOU'RE IN CHARGE!

UNIT NINE OBJECTIVES: How well did you meet the objectives for this unit? Check the box next to each objective you feel you mastered.

GRAMMAR	LISTENING	SPEAKING
❑ Word order in noun phrases ❑ Order of adjectives	❑ Listening for definitions	❑ Explaining steps of a process

PRONUNCIATION	READING	WRITING
❑ Sentence stress and intonation in thought groups	❑ Recognizing literary language such as alliteration, repetition, and onomatopoeia	❑ Developing support paragraphs

LEARNING STRATEGIES: Reflect on your use of learning strategies and thinking skills in this unit. What are some of the strategies you employed? Which ones were most successful for you?

Write your thoughts here.

_____
_____
_____
_____
_____
_____
_____
_____
_____
_____

Unit 9 Learning Strategies

- Using context to understand literary language
- Using context to determine meaning
- Making predictions
- Using graphic organizers
- Sequencing ideas
- Working cooperatively

PRACTICE 1

Complete the questionnaire below with your own information. Work with a partner and write your partner's responses. How do your responses compare? Share your answers with the class.

If you moved to another country, what would you miss most?

What would you miss?	You	Your Partner
Foods		
Holidays		
Family traditions		
Activities		

PRACTICE 2

Use the words in the box to complete the sentences. Refer to page 125 in your student book for help.

> flip-flops
> hobble
> lug
> go on for hours
> pay the price
> get mileage out of
> cart around
> break down

1. I can't believe I brought such a heavy suitcase; now I'll have to _____ it with me for the rest of the trip.

2. Just wait until we get home and tell our story! I'll _____ our nightmare experience with customs at the airport!

3. I have walked so many miles seeing the sights that I can barely _____ to the subway station; my feet are killing me!

4. Oh, no. Here come the Johnsons to show us their vacation photos. I just know they'll _____ about their experiences in Hong Kong.

5. It's a good idea to wear your _____ at the beach since the sand can be extremely hot.

6. If you travel without adequate preparation, you will eventually _____ in discomfort and unpleasant situations.

7. Sonia had to _____ her extra sweaters when the weather turned warm unexpectedly.

8. I guess I should _____ and buy traveler's insurance; it's the safest way to travel.

PRACTICE 3

A. Two neighbors on their way to work are talking about future plans. Work with a partner. Complete the conversation.

ROLES	CONVERSATION	FUNCTIONS
Patricia:	You know, I'd love to be living on my own private island right now.	State a goal or aspiration.
Robert:	Yeah, wouldn't we all. It would sure beat this hot, crowded train. When will you _____?	Show skepticism.
Patricia:	Well, I'm not sure, but I think I'll have saved _____ by the time _____. By then I'll _____.	Explain how you will realize your dream and live your life.

B. Take turns being the neighbors and use the cues to talk about other plans.

a. hike through Ireland **c.** learn to oil paint **e.** (your own idea)

b. start a magazine **d.** build a house

PRACTICE 4

A. Circle the answers that best complete the sentences.

Maria Elena is a travel consultant for several international companies. She makes any and all travel arrangements so that her clients **(1. won't have worried/won't have to worry)** about anything. By the time those clients **(2. need/will have needed)** to travel, Maria Elena **(3. will already give/will already have given)** them sound advice on what to expect on the journey. In June, she **(4. will work/will have been working)** in the travel industry for thirty years. It **(5. will have been/has been)** a joy for her to assist clients whether they were taking business trips or vacations. By the time Maria Elena is ready to retire, she **(6. will be saving/will have been saving)** money her entire working life. What is she hoping to do in retirement? Why travel, of course!

B. Compare your answers with a partner's and explain your choices.

Unit 10

74

PRACTICE 5

What will you have accomplished years from now? Write sentences using the future perfect or future perfect progressive. Share your sentences with the class.

Example: _A year from now, I will have graduated from school._

1. a year from now

   _____

2. five years from now

   _____

3. ten years from now

   _____

4. twenty years from now

   _____

5. thirty years from now

   _____

PRACTICE 6

A. Read each statement and decide if it is **C** (a complete sentence), **F** (a sentence fragment), or **R** (a run-on sentence).

_____ **1.** You wanted me to write about my first impressions of Chicago.

_____ **2.** Your prediction that I would find it fast paced.

_____ **3.** Before I arrived here, my imagination had created amazing visions of this city, I had seen so many pictures of its famous sites.

_____ **4.** My naïve dream that skyscrapers would really scrape the sky.

_____ **5.** My first day here I couldn't wait to rush to the Sears Tower and peer up at its many stories.

_____ **6.** The top was in sight, I could see it easily.

_____ **7.** The building wasn't as imposing as I had imagined, I was quite disappointed.

_____ **8.** Instead of taking the elevator to the top, I preferred to turn away and go walking in the park.

The 110-story Sears Tower Chicago, Illinois

B. Compare your answers with a partner's and explain your choices.

A. Rewrite the paragraphs on the lines below. Correct all sentence fragments and run-on sentences.

1. Nowadays many businesses must think about global issues when trying to market products, one example is a car with the name Nova, meaning "new" in the United States. It did not sell well in Latin America, where *no va* means "doesn't go."

_____

_____

_____

_____

_____

2. Book and magazine covers cannot always be the same in every country and cultural sensitivity must be taken into account for example, using a drawing of people in swimsuits may be inappropriate in some countries or showing an incorrectly drawn Eiffel Tower. May be insulting in France.

_____

_____

_____

_____

_____

3. Tastes in design differ from country to country too. For instance, designers in London feel that the covers of American books. Both novels and nonfiction, are coarse because they do not use much illustration, instead they use big bold type and bright colors. The American view is that British book covers are too weak, gentle, and only slightly attractive.

_____

_____

_____

_____

_____

B. Compare your paragraphs with a partner's.

PRACTICE 8

A. Before You Listen Discuss with a partner. What are some countries you wish to visit? Why? How could you turn this wish into a reality?

Burton Holmes, famous world traveler

B. Listen to a panel discussion about a world traveler and answer the questions.

1. How many Atlantic Ocean crossings did Burton Holmes make?

    _____

2. How many Pacific Ocean crossings did he make?

    _____

3. How many times did Burton Holmes circle the globe?

    _____

4. What were three of the "firsts" that Holmes accomplished?

    _____

    _____

    _____

5. What were three historic events that he attended?

    _____

    _____

    _____

6. What was Burton Holmes's eccentric habit?

    _____

    _____

    _____

C. Compare your answers with a partner's. During what time period do you think Burton Holmes lived?

PRACTICE 9

A. Predict the pronunciation. Underline the stressed syllables and cross out the letters that will be dropped as the sentences are built.

> **A:** You mailed her a ticket.
>
> **B:** If you mailed her a ticket
>
> **A:** If you had mailed her a ticket
>
> **B:** Would you react if you had mailed her a ticket?
>
> **A:** Would you have reacted if you had mailed her a ticket?
>
> **B:** How would you have reacted if you had mailed her a ticket?
>
> **A:** How would you have reacted if you had mailed her a ticket and she tore it up?
>
> **B:** How would you have reacted if you had mailed her a ticket and she tore it up and refused to go?

B. Listen to check your predictions.

C. Work with a partner and take turns reading the sentences.

PRACTICE 10

A. Write **B** (blocking) next to the sentences that might be used to block progress in a discussion.

_____ **1.** Can't anyone pay attention for more than one minute at a time?

_____ **2.** Did I tell you about my last vacation? What a nightmare that was!

_____ **3.** I put my full support behind Marcus's proposal.

_____ **4.** Could that idea possibly be any more irrelevant?

_____ **5.** Would you mind clarifying section four of the report?

_____ **6.** That's the most ridiculous idea yet.

B. Work in small groups. One member of the group should take on the role of blocker. Other members should try to manage the blocking behavior. At the end of the discussion, talk about how the group could further discourage the blocker's behavior. Choose one of the following topics for your discussion.

TOPICS

- Future possibilities for the travel industry
- Eliminating ethnocentrism
- Planning a multicultural festival
- Getting the most mileage from a trip

Read the introduction to a short research paper and answer the questions that follow. Discuss your answers in small groups.

There's No Place Like Home:
Psychological Effects of Frequent Moving on Young Children

In the last fifteen years, research has shown the psychological consequences on young children of home displacement, such as prolonged travel or frequent moves. Just what those effects are, as well as their advantages and disadvantages, are still a matter of controversy.

In general, psychologists agree that young children should accompany their parents when there are frequent moves due to job transfers. However, views differ about the number and types of effects these young children experience. This paper hopes to examine the psychological consequences of home displacement in young children (between four and twelve years old) and address the following: the types of psychological effects currently identified in the literature, how long these effects last, the benefits and drawbacks of these effects, and how these could affect parents' decisions about moving.

---

1. How did the writer shape the introduction? Did it move from more general to more specific information or from more specific to more general information?

_____

_____

2. Where is the thesis statement found? Is this the most effective placement? Why or why not?

_____

_____

_____

3. What audience does the writer of the paper probably have in mind? How do you know?

_____

_____

4. How would you change the introduction, if at all? Why?

_____

_____

_____

YOU'RE IN CHARGE!

UNIT TEN OBJECTIVES: How well did you meet the objectives for this unit? Check the box next to each objective you feel you mastered.

GRAMMAR	**LISTENING**	**SPEAKING**
❑ Future perfect and future perfect progressive tense ❑ Sentence fragments ❑ Run-on sentences	❑ Listening for details	❑ Dealing with communication blocking tactics

PRONUNCIATION	**READING**	**WRITING**
❑ Stress-timing and linking	❑ Recognizing descriptive language	❑ Writing the introduction

LEARNING STRATEGIES: Reflect on your use of learning strategies and thinking skills in this unit. What are some of the strategies you employed? Which ones were most successful for you?

Write your thoughts here.

_____

Unit 10 Learning Strategies

- Using context to determine meaning

- Noting details

- Evaluating

- Making predictions

- Analyzing

- Comparing

- Working cooperatively

WE'RE ALL IN THIS TOGETHER

PRACTICE 1

Sayings about competition and cooperation are found in many languages and cultures around the world. Work in small groups to explain what the following expressions mean. Provide real-life examples for each one. Then share your ideas with the class.

- It takes a whole village to raise a child. (African)
- One hand washes the other. (Yiddish)
- Only when all contribute their firewood, can they build a strong fire. (Chinese)
- Too many boatmen send the boat up the mountain (Korean)

PRACTICE 2

Complete the definitions with words from the box. Refer to page 137 in your student book for help.

1. _____ is the ability to make decisions or take action.

2. Your _____ is someone who lives in the same period of time as you do.

3. To _____ is to try very hard to achieve something.

4. _____ means that responsibility is taken for individual or group actions.

5. To be _____ is to be chosen from among a group to receive special attention.

6. To _____ means to get promotions of increasing responsibility and title.

7. To _____ something means to find the reason or cause.

8. To be _____ means to be controlled by another organization or company.

strive

accountability

singled out

contemporary

taken over

chalk it up to

initiative

move up the corporate ladder

PRACTICE 3

A. A university professor and an exchange student are discussing some of the school's policies. Work with a partner. Complete the conversation.

ROLES	CONVERSATION	FUNCTIONS
Exchange student:	Students in small classes have an advantage over students in large classes. I think that every class for a particular course should have the same number of students.	Complain about a policy.
University professor:	But students choose their own classes, so I don't have any control over how many students are in a class.	Counter the argument.
Exchange student:	Yes, but _____ _____ .	Support your argument.
University professor:	_____ _____	Challenge the supporting information.

B. Take turns being the university professor and the exchange student and discuss your opinions about other situations.

SITUATIONS

a. Some students have to buy their books while other students illegally use photocopies.

b. The school administration cancels classes with no prior notice or refund.

c. Some teachers don't start or finish their classes on time.

d. (Your own idea)

PRACTICE 4

A. Complete the conversation with the appropriate form of the verbs in parentheses.

FATHER: Have you seen Danny's soccer shorts and T-shirt?

MOTHER: I think his shorts **(1. be)** _____ in the dryer, but I don't know where his T-shirt **(2. be)** _____ .

FATHER: Well, Danny's team **(3. expect)** _____ him to meet them in two hours.

MOTHER: Two hours **(4. be)** _____ plenty of time to find his uniform. I'm concerned about something else though. Can we talk for a minute?

FATHER: Sure. What's on your mind?

MOTHER: Well, Danny **(5. seem)** _____ upset a lot of the time when he **(6. come)** _____ home from the games.

FATHER: Yes, that's true. But he's very competitive, and when his team **(7. lose)** _____ he takes it pretty hard.

MOTHER: That's what I mean. Sports **(8. be)** _____ more than competition. I'd like you to talk to Danny about it. Point out the positives, such as the skills he's learning, the exercise he's getting, and the friends he's made.

FATHER: Yeah, people **(9. forget)** _____ about those things. They're important too. I'll be sure to mention that to Danny . . . as soon as I find his uniform.

B. Compare your answers with a partner's and explain your choices.

PRACTICE 5

A. Write **C** (count noun) or **NC** (non-count noun) next to each sentence according to how the boldfaced word is being used.

_____ **1.** A quickly changing market is one of the challenges that **business** faces today.

_____ **2.** I attended my first gymnastics **competition** last week.

_____ **3.** Did you see that great baseball **game** on TV last night?

_____ **4.** **Sports** have become so commercialized in recent years.

_____ **5.** The **competition** for university scholarships is very stiff.

_____ **6.** My uncle opened a new **business** two years ago, and he's already expanded to a second location.

_____ **7.** Gymnastics is rigorous and demanding.

_____ **8.** Though my father was a hunter, my brother never enjoyed hunting **game**.

B. Compare your answers with a partner's and explain your choices.

C. Work with a partner to write new sentences using the boldfaced words as count or non-count nouns on a separate sheet of paper. Share your sentences with another pair.

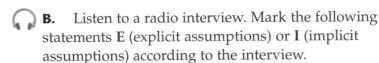

PRACTICE 6

Circle the correct verb and complete the sentences with information of your own. Share your sentences with the class.

1. Politics **(is/are)** _____.

2. Twelve hours **(is/are)** _____.

3. People **(is/are)** _____.

4. The audience **(was/were)** _____.

5. The new-style pants **(is/are)** _____.

6. The Chinese **(has/have)** _____.

7. One hundred dollars **(is/are)** _____.

8. News **(is/are)** _____.

PRACTICE 7

a group of boys in conflict

A.   Before You Listen Discuss with a partner. What causes conflicts between people? Have you ever helped your friends or family to resolve a disagreement? What did you do to help the situation?

B.   Listen to a radio interview. Mark the following statements **E** (explicit assumptions) or **I** (implicit assumptions) according to the interview.

_____ **1.**   Community mediators are trained.

_____ **2.**   A community mediator needs to have a lot of patience.

_____ **3.**   Courts make referrals to mediation.

_____ **4.**   Judges want people to solve their own problems.

_____ **5.**   Mediators might use their intuition to handle the disputants.

_____ **6.**   There are ground rules to follow during a mediation.

_____ **7.**   The mediation process is a long process.

_____ **8.**   Mediation requires cooperation from the disputants.

C.   Work in small groups and discuss these questions.

1.   What do you think are some of the basic rules for a mediation?

2.   What do you think are some qualities that a mediator should have?

3.   Do you think that mediation can be successful in every situation? Why or why not?

A. Predict the sound deletions, additions, or changes in the boldfaced words of the following conversation. Write **D** (deletion), **A** (addition), or **C** (change) above the words.

TEAM CAPTAIN: Okay, everybody, let's pull together and **plan our** strategy. We **have to** C C
 build our robot before the other five teams. C

ANA: I'll gather the materials.

ILHAN: Don't **forget to** get **plenty of screws**, all sizes.

TEAM CAPTAIN: Where's Julio? **Did he go to** look for more tools?

ILHAN: He **just contacted** me on the radio, Cap. He's got the tools.

TEAM CAPTAIN: OK, now we **need to clear** some **space to work**. **Ilhan and** Ana, **can you** move this table **to give us** more room?

ANA: **Let's start** building **as soon as** Julio's here. I see the other **teams are** already busy.

TEAM CAPTAIN: **Don't worry**, Ana. The way we **work together**, nobody will **beat us**.

JULIO: **Sorry I** took so long. I **had to** find a box **to put** the **tools in**.

TEAM CAPTAIN: Let's **get to** work.

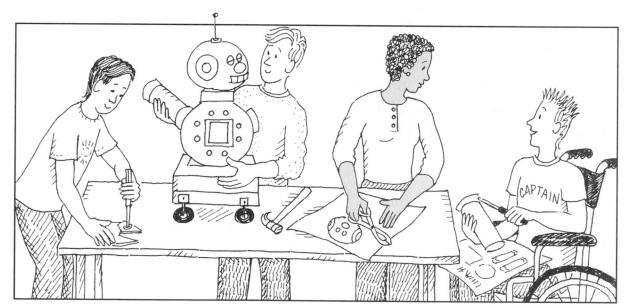

B. Listen to the conversation to check your predictions.

C. Work with a partner and take turns reading the conversation aloud.

PRACTICE 9

A. Mark the following statements **T** (true) or **F** (false) according to what you learned in your student book.

TIPS FOR GIVING A PERSUASIVE TALK

_____ **1.** Ignore arguments that don't favor your side. There's no need to introduce them.

_____ **2.** Share your experiences, goals, or problems as an opener for your talk.

_____ **3.** Don't ask the audience to make a huge shift in their thinking. Ask for a small change.

_____ **4.** Choose a safe topic so there won't be any disagreement.

_____ **5.** Explain why your position is stronger than the other side's.

_____ **6.** At the end of your talk, tell the audience that this is only your opinion and they don't have to change.

_____ **7.** Sound like a reasonable person with an understanding of the audience.

_____ **8.** Don't try to persuade your audience. Just be informative and give examples.

B. Compare your answers with a partner's and explain your choices.

C. Work in small groups. Develop a two to three minute persuasive talk in response to one of the following questions. Take turns giving your talk to the group. Use the note card below to write your ideas.

- Are entrance exams for the university necessary?
- Are cooperative school activities better for learning?
- Do video games encourage unhealthy competition?
- Are team sports competitive or collaborative?
- Should job promotions be based on exams?

Topic:

Opener:

Arguments:

Closing:

Imagine that you are going to write an essay based on one of the statements from the Warm-Up, page 135, Exercise 1, in your student book. Make an outline of your essay below. Then write a full concluding paragraph giving a next step, a new question for further inquiry, an appropriate quotation, or a memorable line.

OUTLINE

Thesis statement:

Support Paragraph 1:

Support Paragraph 2:

Support Paragraph 3:

Conclusion:

YOU'RE IN CHARGE!

UNIT ELEVEN OBJECTIVES: How well did you meet the objectives for this unit? Check the box next to each objective you feel you mastered.

GRAMMAR
❏ Irregular nouns
❏ Collective nouns
❏ Count or non-count nouns

LISTENING
❏ Listening for explicit and implicit assumptions

SPEAKING
❏ Giving a persuasive talk

PRONUNCIATION
❏ Blending and linking words in connected speech

READING
❏ Evaluating an argument

WRITING
❏ Writing the concluding paragraph

LEARNING STRATEGIES: Reflect on your use of learning strategies and thinking skills in this unit. What are some of the strategies you employed? Which ones were most successful for you?

Write your thoughts here.

_____

_____

_____

_____

_____

_____

_____

_____

_____

Unit 11 Learning Strategies

- Using context to determine meaning
- Taking notes
- Evaluating
- Making predictions
- Using graphic organizers
- Classifying
- Working cooperatively

A LAUGHING MATTER

PRACTICE 1

Puns are an amusing use of a word or phrase that has two meanings,
or use of words with different meanings but the same sound.
Write the words or meanings that each of these puns confuses.
Then work with a partner and take turns explaining the pun.

1. An egotist is someone who is always *me-deep* in
   conversation.

   _____

2. A doctor should always keep his temper because he
   can't afford to lose his *patients*.

   _____

3. The butcher put a lot of bread in the sausages because she couldn't make
   both ends *meat*. _____

4. Why is a dog's tail like the center of a tree? Because it's the farthest thing
   from the *bark*. _____

PRACTICE 2

Use the words in the box to complete the sentences. Refer to page 148
in your student book for help.

aerobic
boosts
endorphins
serum
immune
rowing
shrivel

1. A number of scientists have shown that laughter
   _____ the body's ability to fight disease.

2. Muscles _____ and become weaker after long
   periods of inactivity.

3. Our blood consists of red and white blood cells and
   _____, which is the watery part of the blood.

4. When we laugh, natural painkillers in the brain called
   _____ are released.

5. Exercise that increases the oxygen levels in the body is
   called _____.

6. _____ a boat is a good form of exercise.

7. In addition to laughter, eating a healthy diet helps to boost your
   _____ system.

PRACTICE 3

A. A contestant is auditioning for an amateur talent show and needs to perform a routine for the show host. Work with a partner. Complete the conversation.

ROLES	CONVERSATION	FUNCTIONS
Contestant:	Have you heard the joke about the man who wanted to get rid of some ducks that kept following him around?	Set up the joke or story.
Show Host:	No. What happened?	Prompt the joke teller.
Contestant:	He asked his friend to take the ducks to the zoo. A little while later, he saw his friend who still had the ducks so he said, "I thought I told you to take them to the zoo?" His friend replied, "I did. And they liked it so much that now I'm taking them to the movies."	Finish the joke.
Show Host:	_____	Respond to the joke.
Contestant:	_____	Follow up on the response.

B. Take turns being the contestant and the show host and use the cues below.

a. a riddle

b. a pun

c. an amusing story

d. (your own idea)

PRACTICE 4

A. Complete the following sentences with the appropriate form of the possessive.

1. The symphony conductor was rehearsing the second movement **(1.)** _____ Beethoven **(2.)** _____ Ninth Symphony when the violinist **(3.)** _____ cat meowed. The conductor threw down his baton and shouted, "Would the owner **(4.)** _____ that cat please take it out and have it tuned!"

2. Ms. Smith **(5.)** _____ dance class was rehearsing Stravinsky **(6.)** _____ *The Rite* **(7.)** _____ *Spring*. The movements **(8.)** _____ one of the dancers were completely wrong. "What's the matter?" asked Ms. Smith. "Can't you hear the rhythm **(9.)** _____ the music?" "Oh, sure," replied the student. "But I don't let it bother me."

3. The parents **(10.)** _____ a boy who had just gotten his driver **(11.)** _____ license were upset because the boy always wanted to use his father **(12.)** _____ car. He even wanted to drive to the home **(13.)** _____ a friend who lived only two blocks away. "You have two good feet," said the boy **(14.)** _____ mother. "What do you think they're for?" "For the gas pedal and the brake!" the boy replied.

B. Compare your answers with a partner's and explain your choices.

PRACTICE 5

Write an expression of possession for each numbered item and use it as the subject of your sentence. Share your sentences with a partner.

Example: favorite flavor/ice cream

<u>My favorite flavor of ice cream is strawberry.</u>

1. title/favorite movie

_____

2. best friend/favorite hobby

_____

3. mother/favorite color

_____

4. author/favorite book

_____

5. favorite brand/soft drink

_____

PRACTICE 6

A. Complete the sentences with an appropriate time expression from the box.

a moment's	an hour's	three weeks'
a day's	one hundred years'	five years'

1. It's all in _____ work.

2. I'll be spending _____ vacation in Japan.

3. You have to be ready to leave at _____ notice.

4. The criminal was sentenced to _____ hard labor.

5. Gabriel García Márquez writes of _____ solitude.

B. Work with a partner to write a new sentence for each time expression.

PRACTICE 7

A. Before You Listen Work in small groups and take turns giving examples of good humor.

B. Listen to the conversation about humor and laughter. Mark each sentence **T** (true) or **F** (false) according to the conversation.

_____ **1.** Plato and Aristotle thought that humor was good because we should be able to laugh at ourselves.

_____ **2.** Katia feels that humor is positive because it helps people relax and become better acquainted.

_____ **3.** The physical effects of laughing are that it causes a headache and a stomachache.

_____ **4.** Norman Cousins felt that laughter saved his life when he was ill.

_____ **5.** Mr. Cousins believed that positive emotions could produce positive effects on the body.

_____ **6.** Laughing really hard for twenty minutes helped Norman Cousins sleep without pain for ten hours.

_____ **7.** Immediately after Mr. Cousins left the hospital, he went home to write a book.

_____ **8.** Within three weeks' time, Mr. Cousins was without pain and able to go jogging.

C. Listen to the conversation again and mark with an **X** the statements Norman Cousins would probably have agreed with. Discuss your choices with a partner.

_____ **1.** Humans, through determination and training, can control involuntary bodily actions such as blinking.

_____ **2.** Clowns and parties are good for children in hospitals.

_____ **3.** Doctors should realize that the physical action of laughing is dangerous for the seriously ill.

_____ **4.** We should never underestimate the power of the human mind.

_____ **5.** Plato and Aristotle were essentially correct in their assessment of humor.

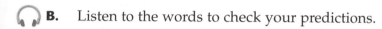

PRACTICE 8

A. Predict where the stress will be in each word by underlining the syllables with the strongest stress.

1.	study	studiously
2.	choreograph	choreography
3.	geography	geographical
4.	fragile	fragility
5.	nation	national
6.	meter	metrical
7.	decide	decision
8.	pronounce	pronunciation
9.	signatory	signature
10.	comic	comedian

B. Listen to the words to check your predictions.

C. Work with a partner and take turns reading the words aloud.

PRACTICE 9

Work in small groups and take turns giving an impromptu talk. To determine your topic, close your eyes and drop a paper clip on the space below. You will talk for one minute on the topic your paper clip falls on. Take a minute to organize the introduction and conclusion in your mind.

The outrageous price of stamps	Someone you know who lacks a sense of humor	Why teenagers should not be allowed to drive	The art of making pizza
Why arranged marriages are best	Ten uses for popcorn	Where all the lost socks go and why	Your first true childhood memory

YOU'RE IN CHARGE!

UNIT TWELVE OBJECTIVES: How well did you meet the objectives for this unit? Check the box next to each objective you feel you mastered.

GRAMMAR
- ❏ Possession: 's and of
- ❏ Parallel structures

LISTENING
- ❏ Listening for supporting details

SPEAKING
- ❏ Making an impromptu speech

PRONUNCIATION
- ❏ Shift of sound and stress in word families

READING
- ❏ Recognizing humor

WRITING
- ❏ Preparing a list of references
- ❏ Revising a research paper

LEARNING STRATEGIES: Reflect on your use of learning strategies and thinking skills in this unit. What are some of the strategies you employed? Which ones were most successful for you?

Write your thoughts here.

_____

Unit 12 Learning Strategies

- Using context to determine meaning
- Taking notes
- Using prior knowledge
- Analyzing
- Making predictions
- Classifying
- Working cooperatively